**Advancing Professional Construction
and Program Management Worldwide**

CONSTRUCTION MANAGEMENT

STANDARDS OF PRACTICE

2021

200 Lawyers Road NW, #1968
Vienna, VA 22183
Phone 703-356-2622 | fax 703-356-6388

www.cmaanet.org

The authors have worked to ensure that all information in this book is correct at the time of publication and consistent with standards of good practice in the construction management industry. As research and practice advance, standards may change. For this reason, it is recommended that readers evaluate the applicability of recommendations considering particular situations and changing standards.

CMAA: Construction Management Association of America
200 Lawyers Road NW, #1968
Vienna, VA 22183

...promoting the profession of Construction Management and the use of qualified Construction Managers on capital projects and programs.

ISBN:978-1-930814-11-6

Printed in the United States of America.

Previous editions: 1986, 1988, 1993, 1999, 2003, 2009, 2010, 2015

Table of Contents

Preface

The *Construction Management Standards of Practice* defines the range of services that constitute professional construction management and serves as an indispensable guide for owners and service providers. This document describes construction management services without limiting the methods and procedures by which a professional construction manager (CM) may provide those services for a particular project or program.

The scope and types of services a CM provides to a specific project or program may vary from those described in this document. This document is intended to provide a menu of services. Not every project/program will require every service, and a particular project/program may require unique services not listed in this document. Whatever service is provided, this document prescribes an industry standard of practice, which the CM will meet or exceed.

CMAA does not intend that this document be used by courts or others to create contractual or legally enforceable duties or requirements, as such duties and requirements are established by terms of the CM's contract and the laws of the jurisdiction in which the CM is practicing. The *Construction Management Standards of Practice* is related to the Standard Forms of Agreement and Contracts published by CMAA. The standard services may change to the extent the provisions of such agreements are modified or altered.

CMAA makes no warranty or representation, including as to accuracy and completeness, regarding the *Standards of Practice*. CMAA disclaims all liability for any harm to persons or property or other damages of any nature whatsoever directly or indirectly resulting from the use of, or reliance on, this document. Adherence to the *Standards of Practice* is not a requirement of CMAA membership or a condition of receipt of any CMAA offering, and CMAA has no authority, nor does it undertake, to monitor or enforce compliance with the *Standards of Practice*. In issuing and making this document available, CMAA is not undertaking to render professional or other services for or on behalf of any person or entity, nor is CMAA undertaking to perform any duty owed by any person or entity to someone else.

The development of this document involved participation by a broad spectrum of the association's membership. Input was gratefully received from industry groups other than CMAA.

Construction Management Standards of Practice is an evolving document, open to scrutiny and critique by the industry. CMAA's leadership is committed to updating and refining the manual to meet the changing needs of CMs and their clients in the years to come.

More details about specific activities and procedures can be found in CMAA's related guidelines, including: *CMAA Claims Management Guidelines, CMAA Contract Administration Guidelines, CMAA Cost Management Guidelines, CMAA Project Closeout Guidelines, CMAA Quality Management Guidelines, CMAA Risk Management Guidelines, CMAA Sustainability Guidelines,* and *CMAA Time Management Guidelines.*

Code of Professional Conduct

The CMAA Code of Professional Conduct represents the aspirations of the profession relative to clients, owners, colleagues, and the public.

"Construction Managers" as used in this Code is a term that applies to CMAA members in performance of their services as Construction and Program Managers. Construction Managers provide a broad range of services to their clients and employers that encompass program, project, and construction management and also serving as owner advisors or representatives.

The code is rooted in the historical values of the profession and linked directly to the CMAA Statement of Values and Policy Framework.

Four fundamental principles form the foundation of the code: Ethical Practice, Professional Excellence, Responsibility to the Public, and Client-Centered Practice.

As a member of CMAA, I/we adhere[i] to the following Code of Professional Conduct:

ETHICAL PRACTICE

1. Construction Managers should be guided in all their relationships by the highest standards of integrity and honesty.
2. Construction Managers should conduct themselves honorably, responsibly, ethically, and lawfully so as to enhance the honor, reputation and value of the profession.
3. Construction Managers should avoid conduct or practices that deceive the public or represent a real or perceived conflict of interest.
4. Construction Managers should respect the rights of others and should not discriminate on the basis of race, color, gender, marital status, religion, national origin, age, disability, or sexual orientation nor knowingly violate any law, statute, or regulation in the performance of professional services. Construction managers should strive to create a diverse workforce.
5. Construction Managers should have a zero-tolerance policy for any form of harassment including sexual harassment and bullying.

PROFESSIONAL EXCELLENCE

6. Construction Managers should perform services only within their areas of competence and qualification.

7. Construction Managers should contribute to the advancement of the program, project, and construction management profession by using best practices, continuing their professional education, and contributing to the development of the future workforce.

RESPONSIBILITY TO THE PUBLIC

8. Construction Managers should hold paramount the health, safety, and welfare of the workplace and the public.

9. Construction Managers should guide and aid in defining and meeting objectives for environmental sustainability and resiliency throughout a project's lifecycle.

CLIENT-CENTERED PRACTICE

10. Construction Managers should ethically represent the best interests of the owner or client, as consistent with this code.

The following is incorporated into internal, CMAA documents.

» *Currently, all CCMs are required to affirm their adherence to the Code of Ethics/Conduct when they renew their certifications.*

» *Further, all CCM and CMIT applicants are required to affirm their adherence to the Code of Ethics/Conduct when they apply for the credential.*

» *This practice continues with the stackable credential.*

» *On April 24, 2020, the Board of Governors approved a motion to require at least 1 ethics or safety education PDH for renewal of the CCM. This is effective January 1, 2021.*

CHAPTER 1

Professional Construction Management

1.1 Introduction

Construction management is the practice of professional management applied to the planning, design, and construction of capital projects from inception to completion for the purpose of achieving project objectives, including meeting all time, scope, cost, and quality goals.

In this document, construction management refers to the application of integrated systems and procedures by a team of professionals to achieve the owner's goals. These systems and procedures are intended to bring each team member's expertise to the project/program in an effective and meaningful manner. The desired result is to achieve a greater benefit from the team's combined expertise than could be realized individually.

This manual addresses program and project organization to achieve the desired results. Professionalism and teamwork are at the core of good construction management. If proper attitudes, goals, commitments, and philosophies are in place, along with an understanding of the expected standards of practice, the procedures required for successful, smoothly executed projects should follow.

Regardless of the project delivery method used (discussed below), good construction management fundamentals and the standards described herein influence the successful outcome of a project or program. As a member of the team, the CM should assume a position of leadership. This should be a position of service, not dominance, which integrates all elements of the project delivery into a cohesive program and begins with the establishment of a management plan.

In addition to an introduction to project delivery methods, this manual addresses the following distinct functions:

1. Professional Construction Management
2. Project Management
3. Cost Management
4. Time Management
5. Quality Management
6. Contract Administration
7. Safety Management
8. Sustainability
9. Technology Management
10. Risk Management
11. Program Management

These functions are not mutually exclusive. They are related and integral components of the construction management process. For ease of reference, functions are presented in the following phases:

- » Pre-design
- » Design
- » Procurement
- » Construction
- » Post-construction

These phases are consistent with the CMAA-suggested scope of services and with established usage for traditional design-bid-build projects in the construction industry.

The CM's scope of services encompasses a broad range of professional skills, management knowledge, and experience. That a CM is certified or licensed in any other profession does not necessarily establish that person as a *qualified* CM. Individuals and firms that provide construction management services should be knowledgeable and experienced in the technical disciplines and management areas described in this manual. CMAA's Certified Construction Manager® (CCM®) certification program represents an industry consensus for the qualifications and experience that identify a professional CM.

1.2   Project Delivery Methods

An agency or owner uses a *project delivery method* as a strategy for a construction project's legal agreements with one or more entities/parties to organize the design, construction, operations, and maintenance services from conception to occupancy. The construction process is a complex undertaking that involves many different activities and people in its planning and execution. A construction project can organize these tasks and the roles/responsibilities of the owner, designer, CM, contractor(s), subcontractor(s), vendors, and suppliers in many ways.

Many approaches exist to deliver a successful project, but it is possible to reduce the number of methods to several basic delivery forms by defining who has responsibility for construction performance, i.e., the actual delivery of the project. These include:

» **Traditional Approach or Design-Bid-Build (D-B-B)**
» **Multiple-Prime Contracting (Multi-Prime)**
» **Construction Management at-risk (CMAR) – also referred to as CM/independent contractor, CM/GC, or CM guaranteed maximum price (GMP)**
» **Design-Build (D-B) – traditional or progressive**
» **Other Methods:** Engineering, Procurement, Construction (EPC); Engineering, Procurement, Construction Management (EPCM); Integrated Project Delivery (IPD); Job Order Contracting (JOC)

Variations of these basic delivery methods are possible depending on the specific needs of the project. Variations may be a function of jurisdictional or statutory requirements. Project participants may also assume multiple roles, resulting in variations in the basic delivery methods. For example, in certain specialty areas such as kitchen design, one firm might serve as the owner's technical advisor, designer, material supplier, and subcontractor at various points during a project.

Common reasons for basic delivery method variations include:

» Different forms of professional and construction contracts
» The degree of care, responsibility, and risk assumed by the parties involved
» Pricing alternatives and methods of compensation
» Fast tracking
» Scope bidding

TRADITIONAL OR DESIGN-BID-BUILD METHOD

The traditional/design-bid-build method remains the most common delivery method for construction projects. Many public sector agencies must only use this method. The parties involved include the owner, the designer, and one or more contractors with subcontractors. The team executes the project's major phases in a linear sequence, requiring the completion of one phase before proceeding to the subsequent phase. The general contractor is normally selected through a low-bid process and does not collaborate in earlier phases.

MULTIPLE-PRIME CONTRACTING

An alternative to the traditional procurement system is multiple-prime contracting, in which the owner holds separate contracts with contractors of various disciplines, such as general construction, structural, mechanical, and electrical. In this system, the owner (often through its CM) administers the contracts and manages the overall schedule and budget during the entire construction phase. Like the traditional method, the owner normally selects contractors through a low-bid process. Sometimes a public owner's procurement regulations also require this method.

Like the CM's role in the traditional approach, the CM acts as the owner's representative toward the prime contractors during construction. However, the CM is typically involved in the design process in this method. The CM's selection is normally through a qualifications-based selection process instead of a low-bid process. Frequently, the ability to start construction before design is complete (i.e., fast track construction) is a goal for this process.

CONSTRUCTION MANAGEMENT AT-RISK

In this method, the CM is generally hired by a qualification-based selection process to provide professional CM services as the owner's agent early in project development. When the design is complete, the CM typically commits to deliver the project within a GMP (usually before the CM solicits bids from subcontractors). There is often a period of negotiations regarding the GMP offer, especially concerning the amount designated for CM contingency.

The owner may accept the CM's offer (at which point the CM transitions to an "at-risk" position), or the owner may decide to end the relationship and place the project out for competitive bid (a process known as the owner taking the "off-ramp"). Advocates for this method cite the construction advantages of the CMAR's involvement in the design phase coupled with the potential for increased cost transparency.

DESIGN-BUILD

The design-build (D-B) project delivery method addresses some of the other methods' limitations. The owner's primary benefit is that only one party is responsible for both the project's design and the execution of construction. Disputes among various project participants remain internal D-B team issues that do not affect the owner. The owner does not act as a referee (or party to blame). This method has gained popularity because more owners want to have a single point of responsibility for their projects to reduce their risk and the potential for disputes.

However, a potential drawback of design-build is that the owner must determine its project requirements first before securing the design-build entity. This avoids delays and additional costs after the design and construction process starts in earnest.

In recent years, a variation of the traditional D-B process has emerged called progressive design-build. "Progressive" refers to the way the owner and design-builder develop the design in a step-by-step progression after the selection of the design-builder.

OTHER METHODS

» **Engineering, Procurement, Construction (EPC)** - EPC is a prominent contracting agreement form used to undertake construction works by the private sector on large-scale/complex infrastructure projects, especially in the energy sector. The engineering and construction contractor will carry out the detailed engineering design of the project, procure all the equipment and materials, and then construct to deliver a functioning facility or asset to their clients. Companies that deliver EPC projects are commonly known as EPC contractors. Normally, the EPC contractor must execute and deliver the project to the "turn of the key" within an agreed time and budget, commonly known as a Lump Sum Turnkey (LSTK) Contract.

» **Engineering, Procurement, Construction Management (EPCM)** - In contrast to the EPC model, the EPCM contractor is not directly involved in the construction of the project but is responsible for the project's detailed design and overall management on behalf of the owner or principal. While an EPC contract takes the form of a design and construction contract, the industry can regard the EPCM model as a professional services contract.

» **Integrated Project Delivery (IPD)** – A project delivery method that contractually requires the primary parties (the owner, the designer, and the builder) to collaborate to collectively manage and appropriately share the risk, responsibility, and liability for project delivery, whether through partnership agreements or multi-party contracts.

» **Job Order Contracting (JOC)** – This delivery method is effective to manage standard construction projects quickly using multi-year contracts or for minor projects, including renovations and repairs. A JOC is a contract with a fixed term or maximum value where one or more contractors are chosen through competitive bids to perform job orders during the contract period.

Delivery Method Considerations

Who has fiduciary responsibility?	Methods of compensation
Will there be an Agency CM?	Financial liabilities
Match competencies to roles	Disclosure of differing legal relationships

1.3   The CM's Role in the Delivery Method

Construction management is a management approach that focuses on the delivery of professional services. There are several different forms and variations of the construction management practice. Each has its own definition, characteristics, and menu of services. All variations can be placed in the "agency" or "at-risk" forms of construction management.

Under an agency approach, the CM may act as the owner's principal agent. The agency CM does not perform design or construction work. The services provided may depend on the owner's in-house resources as well as the services the designer and other consultants provide. All contracts for design, construction, equipment, etc., are directly with the owner. The use of fast tracking, phased construction, or multiple-prime contracts are common but not required.

Under the CMAR delivery method, the CM's role includes the contractual responsibility for construction performance. This approach often occurs under a GMP contract form. The CM will assume additional obligations and will undertake construction responsibilities during the construction phase. At that time, the CM typically enters a legal position like that of a general contractor, i.e., entering into a traditional construction agreement that provides for the completion of the construction work for an established price.

Regardless of the form of contract agreement, the CM performs tasks in a professional capacity throughout all the phases of program/project implementation. A contract agreement will establish the scope of services and define the relationship of the parties. As is intended, the term "agency" implies a delegation of function to the CM by the owner. Consequently, it is possible that certain tasks and responsibilities place the CM in a legal agent relationship with the owner. (See CMAA **Code of Professional Conduct**.)

1.4   Standards of Practice for Delivery Methods

CMAA's *Construction Management Standards of Practice* intends to establish industry service standards and act as a guide for the range of professional construction management services. These standards are intended to apply to construction management professional practice under any project delivery method. Fundamental goals of quality, cost, time, safety, and sound project management apply to all delivery methods. CMAA standards represent specific, sound practices that further those fundamental goals.

These practices apply widely and are recommended regardless of delivery method. The roles of all project participants vary slightly under the different delivery methods, so the party who performs a particular service (or the necessity of a particular service) may vary. The standards defined herein may also apply to multiple parties participating in a project, depending on the delivery method. For example, an agency CM and members of a design-build team may both perform a particular function, such as reviewing quality control procedures during construction.

By issuing this document, CMAA seeks to define construction management services without limiting the methods and procedures by which a professional CM may provide those services for a particular project or program. The scope and types of services a CM provides to a specific project or program may vary from those described in this document. This document is intended to provide a menu of services. Not every project/program will require every service and a particular project/program may require unique services not listed in this document.

Whatever service is provided, this document prescribes an industry standard of practice which the CM is expected to meet or exceed. CMAA does not intend that this document be used by courts or others to create contractual or legally enforceable duties or requirements, as such duties and requirements are established by the terms of the CM's contract and the laws of the jurisdiction in which the CM is practicing. The *Construction Management Standards of Practice* is related to the Standard Forms of Agreement and Contracts which have been published by CMAA. The standard services may change to the extent the provisions of such agreements are modified or altered.

The primary differences in the applicability of these standards to a CM operating as an agent or in different delivery methods are in the procurement, construction, and post-construction stages. The services defined herein for CMs during the pre-design and design stages are provided in a similar manner under all delivery methods, although the contractual responsibilities of each party may be different.

An owner should not delegate certain functions to a CMAR or D-B entity. While the CM plays the primary role in project delivery in CMAR and the design-builder is the primary delivery entity in design-build, the owner should have internal controls and adequate checks and balances to assure sufficient oversight of the project. Functions such as budget establishment and oversight, approval of budget changes (or substantive project changes), and final acceptance of the project should remain within the purview of the owner or that owner's independent designee.

While the D-B or CMAR should perform up to the professional and ethical standards defined herein, prudent management requires that the owner verify the adequacy of the provided professional services. The owner can perform certain functions itself or assign certain verification responsibilities to an independent entity, such as the designer. The owner can also use the services of an agency CM under any delivery method.

CMAR and multiple-prime contracts require additional responsibilities due to the nature of managing various contracting entities. Under Multi-Prime, four or five primes are common and may include as many as twenty or more. On complex CMAR building projects, it is possible to have more than 70 or 80 subcontractors and suppliers.

This document is not intended to address areas such as design, direct supervision/superintendence of work, construction means and methods, and other functions that a CM may perform, particularly those services that might be considered a general contractor's role. For example, a CMAR might be responsible for the selection, procurement, and installation of a concrete formwork system, an aspect of work that might traditionally be a contractor's responsibility.

IPD projects may require a CM to operate in an agency or at-risk capacity. The specifics of the "integrated" approach will vary by the project but may require that the CM enter into agreements that define risk-sharing and cooperation that complement the traditional roles and responsibilities of a CM. Nevertheless, the management principles defined herein will generally apply in IPD formats.

The following table summarizes the applicability of these standards under various delivery methods and construction management concepts.

Delivery Method	CM Type	Comment
Design-Bid-Build (single or multi-prime)	Agency	Some coordination aspects may not apply if using a single general contractor prime contract.
CMAR	At-Risk	The CM will likely have additional responsibilities in terms of administering bonds, managing safety, direct oversight of work, and other elements traditionally within the realm of a general contractor. Some aspects may require additional owner oversight that may be provided by an agency CM, the designer, or the owner's own staff. For example, this may include cost control and final approvals.
Design-Build	Agency	Many sections will not apply, as the Design-Builder will hold the primary responsibility for performance.
Integrated Project Delivery	Agency or At-Risk	Some aspects may be shared with other entities based on the project's specific team structure.

Notes

Notes

CHAPTER 2

Project Management

2.1 Introduction

CMAA defines project management as the use of integrated systems and procedures by a team of professionals during project design and construction. This chapter focuses on the key components and development of a project management plan (PMP) throughout the various project phases. In general, it outlines key goals and elements of managing a project under the construction management format. Later chapters expand upon the approach addressed here.

2.2 Pre-Design Phase

PROJECT ORGANIZATION

During this project phase, the owner must assemble and organize a project team composed of design and construction management professionals as well as other key professional, technical, and administrative staff necessary to assure the project's success. This project team must organize its activities to deliver a project that meets the owner's requirements.

The project team should include the owner, CM, design professional, and any required specialty professionals. In some delivery systems where there is not a CMAR involved, the general contractor may be part of the pre-design team.

The owner should determine and document the basic project purposes, goals, and parameters of performance (particularly cost, time, and quality). The project team should receive these at the earliest opportunity. The CM may need to help facilitate this process, especially with first-time owners.

The terms "project manager" and "CM" are often used in different ways. In this chapter, "CM" refers to the agency construction manager and is interchangeable with the project manager (PM).

In general, these roles apply to a construction manager at-risk as well (aspects limited to a CMAR are addressed specifically).

The owner should hire the CM and design professionals as early as possible. In situations where the CM is hired first, the owner can benefit from having the CM participate in the selection of a design firm. The CM helps the owner develop a list of qualified design firms, develop/transmit the requests for proposals, review the proposals, conduct interviews, evaluate candidates, and make recommendations for the design contract award. When the design professional is hired first, they may assist the owner with CM selection.

The following principles guide project organization:

» The CMAA document *An Owner's Guide to Project Delivery Methods* recommends procedures for the CM selection process.

» The owner, design professional, and CM must establish a relationship of mutual trust and respect. The design professional and CM have distinct roles/responsibilities but function as equals, so the owner should treat them so to gain the team's full collective effort.

» Before signing individual contracts, each team member must understand the overall project requirements and the other members' responsibilities. The best way to accomplish this is to perform a joint review with all parties' respective contracts. The owner, CM, and design professional should then create a responsibility matrix that documents all tasks, action items, and authorities of all team members.

PROJECT MANAGEMENT PLAN (PMP)

The PMP outlines how to accomplish the project requirements and how to measure the project team's performance. It is critical that all team members understand this document from the outset and that it remains updated throughout the project. The CM prepares the PMP in conjunction with the owner and design professional. The owner should then review and approve the PMP before the project proceeds.

The PMP typically establishes the project's:

» Scope
» Budget
» Schedule
» Environmental conditions
» Basic systems
» Methods and procedures
» Basis for claims avoidance

The PMP and the commitment of all stakeholders to meet its requirements form the foundation for a successful project. The owner's time, cost, and performance requirements may require many conceptual design/estimating iterations. However, after the owner approves these requirements the team must commit to complete the project within those expectations.

Typically, a combination of conceptual drawings, descriptive narratives, performance parameters, and the project budget document the project scope. The type of information and amount of detail may vary considerably, based upon the type of project.

Documentation of overall cost and time is the CM's responsibility, with input from the other team members. The establishment of basic systems and procedures by the CM links the task elements of the PMP.

Additional components may be developed in later phases of the project as part of the construction management plan (CMP). A typical PMP includes the following basic components:

- » Project description
- » Scope of work
- » Milestone schedule
- » Master schedule
- » Quality management approach
- » Safety management plan
- » Reference to project documents
- » Project organization chart and staffing plan
- » Explanation of roles, responsibilities, and authority of team members
- » Project budget/work breakdown structure
- » Sustainability plan
- » Logistics, including temporary construction support requirements (i.e., laydown or marshaling area)

- » Environmental/archaeological considerations
- » Reference to project procedures manual
- » Management information system
- » Communications protocol (establish ground rules)
- » Bid packaging, contracting strategy, and delivery system evaluation
- » Site mobilization and utilization phase
- » Building Information Modeling (BIM) implementation strategy

PROJECT PROCEDURES MANUAL

The CM drafts and edits the Project Procedures Manual with input from the team. The PMP clearly defines the team members' responsibilities, levels of authority, communication protocol, and the systems, methods, and procedures for project execution.

The manual should address the following:

- » Cost controls and systems required for monitoring and controlling project costs
- » Quality control and quality assurance program established by the team and how it is to be implemented
- » The project schedule and how it is to be developed, implemented, and maintained
- » Document control and specific project systems, methods, and procedures (i.e., bidding, payments, change orders, submittals, correspondence, reports, performance records, claim resolutions, etc.)
- » Functional responsibilities and limits of authority
- » Correspondence distribution matrix

- » Safety program
- » Checklists
- » Meetings listing (i.e., type, frequency)
- » Sample forms to be used
- » Detailed bidding and construction phase processes
- » Coordination among various prime contractors
- » Sustainability requirements
- » Risk and risk register
- » Regulatory requirements

PRE-DESIGN PROJECT CONFERENCE

Before design begins, the CM plans, conducts, and documents a pre-design project conference that addresses the PMP's design phase considerations. The purpose of the conference is to:

» Define standards for design construction documentation.

» Set primary methods of project documentation/communication.

» Define relationships with the community/other impacted stakeholders.

» Achieve commitment to the project goals and procedures from the owner, design professional, and CM.

MANAGEMENT INFORMATION SYSTEM

The CM establishes a management information system (MIS) that will inform the team of the project's overall status and forecast for comparison to the PMP. The CM facilitates implementation of a web-based MIS unless the owner directs or prefers differently. The system should provide a reliable basis to manage the project as well as identify and evaluate problem areas or variances.

This collaborative system should address team information needs, data sources, and control elements for time and cost. The project should establish policies for information distribution, frequency of reports, and record retention.

The project can achieve a comprehensive account by maintaining records of the following:

» General correspondence files (in and out)
» Periodic reports (daily, weekly, monthly)
» Drawing schedules, submittals (shop drawings, payments, samples)
» Financial status / cost
» Transmittals
» Requests for Information (RFI)
» Requests for Proposals
» Change requests and authorizations
» Procurement
» Material control
» Meeting minutes
» Confirmation of oral instructions and field directives
» Controlled inspections
» Notice of non-conforming contract work
» Weather conditions
» Scheduling records
» Progress photographs

Both the owner and CM must be able to use financial status reports from the MIS to control the available project funds. The MIS should format reports in a way that allows continuous data input throughout the project. This data should serve as a budgeting and cost control tool for individual project phases and the total project.

Financial reporting should cover the following:

- » Budgeted, authorized, and committed funds
- » Expenditures to date
- » Cost to complete
- » Invoices
- » Payments/retention
- » Change orders
- » Projected total costs
- » Projected cash flow

The CM coordinates with the owner and the designer's staff to determine the format and frequency of reports required. Information should include schedule and progress reporting, drawing schedules, budget versus cost of services, and change requests (approved and pending) for design services. The system should issue the first reports during the pre-design phase and thereafter on an agreed frequency.

2.3 Design Phase

During design, the team must continuously consult on all substantive issues. As the process proceeds from schematic through final design, the team must consider each phase's critical issues, moving from general decisions in the early phase to detailed decisions as the design progresses.

The CM should conduct periodic design phase reviews. The owner and the CM should agree on the scope and number of design phase reviews required. The CM coordinates with any needed value engineering and alternative studies. The goal is to develop a complete set of documents that clearly define the scope of a project, which can then be bid in the current local marketplace within the owner's budget and time requirements.

During this phase, the CM carries out the activities listed below to assist the team. The design professional has responsibility for design implementation and execution to meet the project requirements, but the owner (as well as the CM and other stakeholders) will also have decision-making responsibility. Decisions on construction contracting strategies should be complete by the start of design so the designer can execute the work accordingly.

DESIGN DOCUMENT REVIEW

The CM reviews the design documents periodically, focusing on the 5 C's:

1. Clarity
2. Completeness
3. Constructability
4. Compliance (with owner's program)
5. Coordination (among the trades and contractors as appropriate)

Often, the CM will conduct a constructability review using the specifications in the design documents for phasing, logistics, and avoidance of construction conflicts.

DOCUMENT DISTRIBUTION

The CM coordinates the distribution of information among all team members and the transmission of all documents to regulatory agencies.

CONTRACT AGREEMENTS

The owner may ask the CM to review appropriate construction contract agreements for inclusion in the bid documents. (For complete details, see *CMAA Contract Administration Guidelines*.)

GENERAL AND SUPPLEMENTARY GENERAL CONDITIONS

The CM develops or reviews general and special conditions consistent with project requirements.

PUBLIC RELATIONS

The CM assists the owner with public relations, particularly those with the owner's organization and community relations. The CM may help the owner coordinate public review, impact studies, and public design review, as well as develop interest among bidders for the project(s).

PROJECT FUNDING

The CM may help the owner prepare necessary documents to secure funding for the overall project.

MEETINGS, WORKSHOPS, CHARETTES

The CM conducts periodic project meetings to assess progress, verify adherence to the PMP, document performance, plan for completion, and take action to resolve current problems.

At a minimum, these meetings should happen at the end of each design phase. The team should conduct a final review before the release of each bid package. Recommended subjects for each project meeting include:

» Reviewing the project budget and an estimate of construction costs based on the current drawings and specifications, making allowances and assumptions for detail not shown or known.
» Reviewing the project's master schedule, milestone schedule, and any additional detailed sub-schedules.
» Discussing and resolving any unresolved issues which have become evident through the previous review of documents or team discussion.

COST MANAGEMENT

During design, the CM develops and maintains cost control procedures to monitor and control project expenditures (both current and projected) within the allocated budget. Cost control measures will include cost estimates at each design phase and value analysis/value engineering studies.

TIME MANAGEMENT

The CM develops, implements, and periodically updates the master schedule and the milestone schedule to reflect actual performance to date during design. The CM also establishes forecast dates for the completion of the project and advises the owner and designer of performance in relation to that baseline. (See *CMAA Time Management Guidelines*.)

SUSTAINABILITY/RESILIENCY COMPLIANCE

Either the CM (or a qualified sustainability professional) shall provide guidance and oversight during design to ensure the team addresses established sustainability goals. This may include adding commissioning and certification requirements into the milestone/master schedules.

ONGOING CONSULTING ACTIVITIES

The CM makes recommendations to team members regarding constructability, cost, phasing, sequencing of construction, construction duration, the impact of alternative construction methods, and separation of contract categories.

At the end of the design phase, designated representatives of each team member review all design documents and agree that they are complete, coordinated, representative of the owner's needs, and suitable for construction.

2.4 Procurement Phase

Specific procurement activities will vary depending on the project delivery method in use. However, the goal in this phase is to secure bidders for each bid package (or subcontractor trade) who are qualified, competitive, interested in the work, and capable of doing the work within the project time requirements.

BIDDING AND CONTRACTING PROCESS

The CM is responsible for performing or helping the owner with several procurement phase activities, which will vary depending on whether the CM is operating in an agency or at-risk capacity.

An agency CM's responsibilities would typically include the following:

» Solicitation and prequalification of bidders, as well as developing the guidelines to evaluate bidders
» Notices and advertisements
» Bidders' interest campaign
» Delivery of bid documents
» Information to bidders
» Issuance of addenda
» Bid opening, evaluation, and recommendation
» Monitoring compliance with and execution of construction contracts
» Arrangement for owner-purchased equipment and materials
» Provision for permits, insurance, and labor affidavits

A CMAR will follow a similar process of dividing the work into appropriate scope packages, separately soliciting bids, and awarding subcontracts for the various scope elements. The awarding of contracts may require owner approval. Additional CMAR responsibilities include the following:

» Develop trade subcontract solicitation list

» Prequalify trade subcontractors

» Develop trade subcontract package recommendations and scopes of work

» Develop MBE, WBE, DBE, small business, etc. solicitation list based on project goals

» Perform pre-bid conference meetings for each trade subcontractor

» Identify long lead equipment and initiate early procurement

» Establish the GMP

» Monitor trade subcontractor bid bonds

MEETINGS

The following meetings may be part of the bid and award process:

» Pre-bid meetings

» Bid openings

» Pre-award conferences

BID ANALYSIS AND NEGOTIATION

The owner may task the CM to tabulate all bids received and prepare a bid analysis. The bid tabulation method should be consistent with previous cost estimates. Based on the bid documents, the analysis should include the evaluation of all alternate bids and unit prices in comparison with the final estimate of construction cost.

The CM's cost management role during this stage is to evaluate, tabulate, and establish that the bids are fully responsive to the requirements of the construction documents and meet the expectations of the construction budget. This may include a descope meeting with qualified bidders to ensure balance and validation of scope before making a recommendation to the owner.

2.5 Construction Phase

The construction phase's goal is to expedite and improve the efficiency of the construction process through professional planning and execution of project activities to fulfill the owner's scope, cost, quality, and time requirements.

Before construction, the CM develops a project-specific CMP that clearly identifies the roles, responsibilities, and authority of the project team as well as the procedures for construction.

ON-SITE FACILITIES

The CM verifies that the project provides office facilities, site work required for general access, and utilities to all on-site organizations. The cost of the work may be paid directly by the owner or by the CM as a reimbursable cost. Alternatively, individual construction contracts may include some or all the work.

COORDINATION

The CM provides coordination and leadership of the individual professionals and contractor(s) to meet the project requirements. To help accomplish this, all communications with professionals and contractor(s) are either through the CM or with the CM's prior knowledge. The owner, design professional, and individual contractor(s) should follow the established formal lines of communication.

MEETINGS

There are three basic meeting categories in the construction phase: pre-construction, progress, and special meetings.

1. Pre-construction meetings review project procedures, site utilization requirements, and near and long-term activity plans with all on-site contractors. The CM discusses a comprehensive list of contract requirements, including the lines of communication, shop drawing procedures, and general written communication protocol.

2. Progress meetings monitor compliance with schedules and the requirements of the contract documents. They coordinate contractor efforts and allow short to mid-term planning/problem-solving. The CM organizes, conducts, and records regularly scheduled progress meetings which include the CM, contractor's principal personnel, design professionals, and owner, as required. Meetings may happen weekly, every two weeks, or at least once a month.

3. Special meetings resolve issues of an immediate or short-term nature that should not wait until the regularly scheduled progress meetings or that involve issues not suitable for the progress meeting. Examples of special meetings include safety incident response, pre-submittal, and pre-installation. Regardless of the topic, the meeting should be brief and focus on the identified issue. Although the CM has primary responsibility for these meetings, the owner, designer, or contractor may call a special meeting through the CM.

TIME MANAGEMENT

The CM establishes procedures for planning and monitoring compliance with the project schedule relative to the overall project master schedule. These procedures should include reviews of the detailed construction schedule at appropriate time intervals (typically monthly).

This process should also consider the on-site contractors in the development and updates to project schedules. The CM obtains a commitment from each contractor to complete the project within the owner's time requirements as required by the contract documents, provides the contractor with the required critical dates, and then monitors compliance with the detailed project schedule.

When schedule delays occur or may occur, the CM works with the contractor to identify appropriate opportunities to recover. If time-related contract claims arise, the time management process forms the basis for evaluating and resolving them.

COST MANAGEMENT

The CM is responsible for monitoring and forecasting costs for the owner during the construction phase. As contracts are awarded, the individual line-item estimates are replaced with actual committed amounts, plus cost estimates for any unknowns or contingencies. The goal is to monitor and manage the incurred costs, estimated costs, and costs to complete to stay within the budget. (See *CMAA Cost Management Guidelines.*)

PAYMENT REQUESTS

The CM implements procedures for processing contractors' payments per the contract requirements. The CM should schedule monthly meetings to review and discuss pay requests.

CHANGE ORDERS

The CM leads the project team's documented procedures for initiating and approving contractor change orders. All cost issues that will potentially impact the total project costs should be documented and tracked until fully dis-positioned by the project team.

CLAIMS MANAGEMENT

The CM establishes procedures to minimize claims' impact on the ongoing construction effort through prompt and equitable resolution. Procedures should address reception and disposition of submitted claims, merit evaluation, entitlement evaluation, negotiation and settlement, handling of disputes, and appeals. All claims and potential claims should be discussed at the progress meetings. (See *CMAA Risk Management Guidelines.*)

QUALITY MANAGEMENT

In most cases, the construction contractor is responsible for the quality control function and compliance with the quality required by the contract documents.

The CM monitors the contractors' compliance with the quality expectations defined during the pre-design phase. The CM's contract should clearly spell out the CM's responsibilities for quality control or quality assurance. With a knowledge of the construction contract and project roles, the CM has the tools to respond to any quality issues that may arise.

The CM arranges to field test any aspects of the work with unusual testing requirements that do not fall within the contractor's work scope. This may include coordinating required inspections with the owner and designer stakeholders.

ACCEPTANCE AND PERFORMANCE TESTING

If required by the contract, the CM monitors the acceptance and performance testing to see that it meets the contract requirements. The contractor will need to provide an opportunity for the CM to observe these tests as well as file all appropriate test reports. Third-party commissioning agents may help to perform this function.

FINAL INSPECTION AND PUNCHLISTS

After a written request from the contractor, the inspection staff will consider if the contract work is substantially complete and will conduct a final inspection with the contractor, design team, project staff, and owner's representatives.

During the final inspection, the CM develops the project punchlist of the remaining contract work. If the designer and CM recommend that the remaining items are not critical to occupancy or use, the owner declares the contract substantially complete. The CM must monitor the completion of the remaining punchlist items, which the contractor should complete in the time frame specified in the bid documents. Upon the punchlist completion, the CM will issue a final inspection report.

OWNER OCCUPANCY (PARTIAL ACCEPTANCE/BENEFICIAL OCCUPANCY)

After the owner declares the contract substantially complete and receives a Certificate of Occupancy (CO) from permit inspections, the CM helps the owner take beneficial occupancy of the project. This may occur in phases for larger projects and include filing the appropriate reports and approvals before governing boards or other owner representatives. In certain circumstances, partial acceptance can be taken for project elements that are substantially complete.

OWNER-PURCHASED MATERIALS AND EQUIPMENT

Before construction, the CM identifies materials and equipment for pre-purchasing that are long lead or that could be directly purchased to the owner's advantage. As per the contract, the CM typically coordinates scheduling, on-site delivery, storage, installation, and startup requirements for these materials and equipment.

RECORD DRAWINGS, MODELS, AND DOCUMENTS

The contractor doing the work should provide record and BIM drawings. During construction, the CM monitors the record drawing process monthly as part of the review of contractor applications for payment. The CM also receives these drawings at the completion of construction. The CM must also maintain redline documents and monitor them regularly with payment applications.

DOCUMENT CONTROL

The CM establishes systems to ensure a smooth, efficient, and prompt flow of all project-related paperwork that includes modern information technology. (See **Chapter 9: Technology Management**.)

MANAGEMENT REPORTING

The CM should establish a management reporting system in pre-design and maintain it throughout the project to keep all team members informed on the project's status. The CM determines the type, format, frequency, and distribution of information and reports required in accordance with the CMP and the Project Procedures Manual.

RISK AND SAFETY MANAGEMENT

The CM methodically applies risk management processes to reduce the negative impact of uncertainties on a project's cost, schedule, and quality expectations.

Depending on its contractual status (agency or at-risk), the CM reviews the contractor's safety plan but may or may not be responsible for implementation or compliance. It is essential to develop a system that periodically evaluates the contractor's compliance with its safety plan and prepares a formal report of the results. The CM's CMP should outline these procedures.

SUSTAINABILITY MANAGEMENT

The CM should understand the project's sustainability goals and establish a tracking system to monitor compliance. Commissioning for sustainability certification is associated with acceptance and performance testing. When the project retains an independent commissioning agent, the CM oversees the commissioning process in coordination with the project designer. Otherwise, the commissioning process is the CM's responsibility. During commissioning, the CM must complete and submit all sustainability documentation for certification of points that are obtainable during the construction process and in accordance with contract documents.

2.6 Post-Construction Phase

Project closeout must be quick and effective for a successful project. Depending on the contract, the CM's responsibility in the post-construction phase may include the following:

» Obtaining sustainability certification, if applicable
» Completion of punchlist items not required for substantial completion
» Facilitating owner occupancy
» Assembling record drawings for as-built documentation
» Warranty, guarantee, and operation and maintenance manuals
» Pursuing resolution of warranty items

- » Documentation of final pay quantities and costs
- » Preparing contract files for transfer to the owner
- » Final payment and contract acceptance
- » Auditing or full audit report
- » Release of liens
- » Final deductive/additive change orders

(Also see *CMAA Project Closeout Guidelines*.)

ASSEMBLING RECORD DOCUMENTS, DRAWINGS, AND MODELS FOR AS-BUILT DOCUMENTATION

The CM must ensure that the owner receives accurate and timely as-built drawings and specifications as soon as possible after the completion of construction. The contractor maintains record drawings which the CM should inspect monthly during construction. The owner or design team receives these record drawings for the generation of the as-built documentation.

WARRANTY, GUARANTEE, AND OPERATION AND MAINTENANCE MANUALS

The CM must define and document when the warranty periods begin, then ensure that all warranty, guarantee, and operation and maintenance (O&M) manuals comply with contract requirements, and finally submit these to the owner before project closeout. If required, the CM oversees any specialized training by the contractor, which usually must occur before the project's formal acceptance. (See *CMAA Project Closeout Guidelines*.)

WARRANTY ADMINISTRATION

If requested by the owner, the CM uses a calendar to plan expiration inspections to resolve all warranty issues. These issues may include an evaluation of whether the issue is actually a warranty issue, notification of the prime contractor or appropriate suppliers, and verification that warranty work is satisfactorily completed.

DOCUMENTATION OF FINAL PAY QUANTITIES AND COSTS

The CM must compile documentation to report and record final project costs. Documentation must be sufficient for audit purposes.

PREPARING CONTRACT FILES FOR TRANSFER TO OWNER

The CM must prepare the contract files in accordance with the owner's requirements to facilitate their transfer to the owner for archiving.

FINAL PAYMENT AND CONTRACT ACCEPTANCE

The CM helps the owner to accept the contract as complete and process final payments to all parties.

FINAL PAYMENT AND CLOSING OF THE CONTRACT

The CM assembles all final payment documents for the owner's approval, including retention, unresolved change orders, and unpaid invoices. Upon approval of the final payment, all outstanding financial obligations with the contractor are resolved, the payment processes, and the contract closes. If the contractor requests any claims or adjustments, the contract is not closed until these are completely resolved.

Notes

CHAPTER 3

Cost Management

3.1 Introduction

This chapter presents guidelines for the CM to lead and help team members manage, monitor, and report project costs during all project phases through an integrated and comprehensive cost management system.

Effective cost management involves:

» Establishing a realistic and consistent project budget within the owner's available funding.

» Ensuring the project budget is controlled and provides the best, timely information to the owner throughout the project.

Cost management must support the project's lifecycle cost plan and comply with the project's, owner's, and other stakeholders' legal requirements.

The cost management system should be consistent with the project work breakdown structure and compatible with the owner's code of accounts and other stakeholders' requirements, where practical. It should reflect the owner's and CM's need to obtain and communicate cost information to various stakeholders in a timely manner.

Beyond the traditional design-bid-build delivery method, other delivery methods require communicating and aligning the owner's budget and project work breakdown structure to the CMAR contractor, the design-build team, or multiple-prime contractors. These methods may also require the owner to provide higher-level summary cost information to various funding sources, whether private or public.

PRELIMINARY COST INVESTIGATION

The CM assembles a cost management plan with all cost components for approval by the owner, the design professional, and other involved stakeholders. Each party approves the cost plan, which is then the basis to control project costs throughout the design and construction process. The CM should provide the cost management plan as a narrative so that the team clearly understands the basis of the cost management plan along with assumptions, inclusions, exclusions, risks, and other factors that influence the cost management plan.

3.2   Pre-Design Phase

Before the CM develops any construction cost data, they visit the site of the proposed project (if possible) and investigate factors likely to affect construction operations and project costs such as access, wetlands constraints, and existing structures and utilities.

In addition, the CM assesses the construction market and investigates the potential project risks. The CM may conduct a local market survey to determine current costs, availability of labor, materials and equipment, current and future bidding climates, local code requirements, planning/zoning requirements, and other related factors. The CM also conducts an initial analysis of risks that may negatively influence the project along with possible opportunities. The risk management plan documents those issues. (See **Chapter 10: Risk Management**.)

Constructability review and value engineering are not specific to the cost management plan but are also skills that an experienced CM brings to the project.

A construction cost database of similar projects or project elements provides a basis for parametric cost modeling. The database is typically from local historical project records and includes specified project labor rates, if applicable. A database of historical cost information coupled with site-specific knowledge and an understanding of local construction economics enables the CM to confidently begin estimating project construction costs. This reliable project data may also help future projects.

PROJECT AND CONSTRUCTION BUDGETS

The CM develops an estimate of the construction cost based on the owner's performance, quality, and time constraint goals. If possible, the CM compiles an estimate of the total project cost, specifying the basis of each estimate. The CM incorporates this information into the PMP.

The project team has few details during the early project phases. The CM typically only has general details at the budget estimate stage, so they may use a construction contingency. However, estimates are difficult to develop at any stage of a project.

One risk analysis approach is to brainstorm every possible negative event during the project's planning, design, construction, or startup. Then the team develops a probability of each risk occurring, rough order of magnitude costs if that event did occur, or the cost of mitigating that risk before it occurs. Finally, the project team ranks the probability of event occurrence using a classic risk calculation.

$$\text{Expected Monetary Value of Risk} \times \text{Risk Event Probability} = \text{Risk Event Value}$$

The CM informs the owner that the current estimated construction cost is based on data available at this stage of the project. The ultimate cost of the proposed project depends on the quantity and quality of systems yet to be defined.

Work breakdown structures in formats that are consistent with project components and acceptable to the project team are the basis for cost estimates in project and construction budgets.

The CM reviews the budget for completeness, compatibility with any established cost limitations, and attainability. The CM reviews the findings with the owner, design professional, and project stakeholders to make necessary design, program, schedule, or budget adjustments to conform to owner requirements.

A basis of estimate narrative must accompany the budget. It is best practice to note the specific documents and dates used for the basis of estimate. The narrative should clearly identify and discuss any assumptions, clarifications, inclusions, or exclusions made in preparing the project and construction budgets. The CM should also start documenting risks and opportunities inherent in the project.

COST ANALYSIS

During a project's pre-design phase, the owner may ask the designer to develop conceptual design alternatives based on different site locations or project schemes. The CM prepares cost estimates for these alternatives for the owner and designer's review. A consistent, compatible cost estimate format facilitates a timely cost comparison and discussion. Any alternatives that are included in bidding documents should be structured as add alternatives as opposed to deduct alternatives. This typically enables better procurement value for the project.

When considering different sites, the CM should recognize the constraints/impacts of the cost differentials for the following:

- » Utilities
- » Soil conditions
- » Topography
- » Access
- » Location
- » Market conditions
- » Labor

The owner at this stage may also request other studies, including lifecycle cost studies, energy studies, and preliminary cash flows. The CM should present all such studies in reports and review them with the owner, design professional, and other stakeholders.

PRELIMINARY DESIGN ESTIMATE

The CM prepares a preliminary design cost estimate based on measurement of approximate or parameter quantities from the design professional's preliminary design submittal. As the mechanical/electrical designs typically follow the architectural/structural designs, preliminary design estimates often contain approximate quantities for the architectural/structural/civil works and parameter quantities for the mechanical/electrical components.

3.3 Design Phase

Cost management should be proactive during design. The CM should provide timely cost information and work with the design team to reduce the need for redesign from cost overruns.

This requires communication with the design team to predict impending expenditures and stay on budget. Depending on the project delivery method, the contractor's estimators might also be part of this early design cost team.

ESTIMATES

Following the construction budget approval, the CM provides ongoing cost management services to ensure that the designer adheres to the budget as the design develops.

The project team establishes and maintains a consistent cost estimating framework from pre-construction through post-construction. A consistent framework facilitates reliable cost reporting and the ready identification of cost variances as the design develops. This is especially true in CMAR, where the owner and contractor work as a team to reach an agreed construction budget.

Cost Estimates

- ✓ A predicted cost of constructing the project
- ✓ Level of accuracy id dependent upon the quantity and the quality of information available to the estimator
- ✓ Application of quantity surveys to cost estimating
- ✓ Accurate prediction of the project cost
- ✓ The estimate should be neither optimistic nor pessimistic
- ✓ CM should set forth all relevant cost assumptions

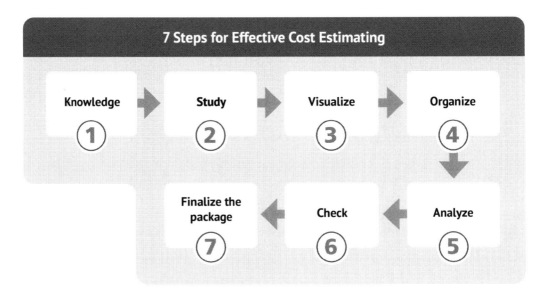

7 Steps for Effective Cost Estimating

Knowledge 1 → Study 2 → Visualize 3 → Organize 4

Finalize the package 7 ← Check 6 ← Analyze 5

The CM prepares estimates to the level of detail available on the drawings and specifications, supplemented by notes and verbal data the owner or designer provide.

All verbal data should be confirmed in writing and noted in the estimate. The estimate narrative should also communicate any significant data.

Cost data at the conceptual, schematic, and design development stages is usually provided on a parameter basis by element and project type. Since these data are usually historical, they should be adjusted or normalized for time, location, scale, and other factors that influence costs.

During the preliminary design and final design document phases, a deterministic estimate with cost data at a unit price level may be more appropriate. This involves quantity takeoff and unit pricing of the individual components of the trade or element (i.e., concrete, reinforcing steel, forms, etc.). The data should be reviewed, verified, and adjusted as necessary before use.

Types of Estimates and Accuracy

RITZ	
ESTIMATE TYPE	ACCURACY
Feasibility	+/- 25-30%
Appropriation	+/- 15-25%
Capitol Cost	+/- 10-15%
Definitive	+/- 5%

AACEI	
ESTIMATE TYPE	ACCURACY
Order of Magnitude	+50% to -30%
Budget	+30% to -15%
Definitive	+15% to -5%

Figure 1: RITZ and AACEI are two examples of cost estimation methods and the accuracy of their estimating factors.

Documents often present unit prices as composite rates inclusive of labor, materials, and equipment. However, many projects also require quantities to be presented with separated labor, material, and equipment pricing. CM's may utilize computer spreadsheets, estimating software programs, and company or agency historical estimating databases to facilitate the organization, sorting, and presentation of cost estimates. This also facilitates the ability to report cost information in different formats for analysis.

When developing estimates of construction cost during the design phase, the CM refers to all available contract documents, including the plans, specifications, and contract-referenced material. The CM should carefully study specifications since they provide information which the drawings may not show and that may have cost impacts.

Costs should reflect current market pricing, with escalation addressed as a separate and distinct line item. There are a variety of industry sources that provide cost escalation rates and forecasting data. Escalation cost estimates should be computed based on a monthly rate from the date of the estimate to the midpoint of construction. As the project moves into the construction document phase, the escalation may be refined by escalating major components of the project in accordance with the procurement schedule.

The owner should agree to the escalation rate. All estimates should communicate the escalation rate clearly and consistently.

COST VERIFICATION STAGES

To verify that the project remains within the construction and project budgets, the CM prepares estimates at the following stages of the design process:

» Completion of schematic design

» Completion of preliminary design

» Completion of the design development phase

» In progress final design (may vary from 60–90% complete)

» Completion of bid documents (including any issued addenda)

The CM evaluates each project based on its unique conditions and the above-named characteristics. Each cost verification stage should have set design contingencies.

The design contingency level reflects the level of accuracy that it is reasonable to expect from estimates at each project stage. The project team determines the percentage allowable for design and construction contingencies on an individual project basis.

The Association for the Advancement of Cost Engineering (AACE) presents five estimate classes:

Estimate Class	Maturity Level of Project Deliverables	Typically Expected Accuracy Range	Preparation Effort
Class 5	0% to 2%	-50% to +1000%	1
Class 4	1% to 15%	-30% to +50%	2 to 4
Class 3	10% to 40%	-20% to +30%	3 to 10
Class 2	30% to 75%	-15% to +20%	5 to 20
Class 1	65% to 100%	-10% to +15%	10 to 100

For more on estimating, see *CMAA Cost Management Guidelines*.

SCHEMATIC DESIGN ESTIMATE

The CM prepares a schematic design cost estimate based on parameter quantity measurements from the designer's schematic design stage submittal. It may also be possible to measure approximate quantities for certain project elements. A design-build contractor often joins the project team at this phase.

IN PROGRESS AND FINAL DESIGN DOCUMENT ESTIMATES

Cost estimates prepared from working drawings and specifications are based on quantity estimates for all major components. Any alternatives called for in the bid documents should be quantified and estimated. A CMAR contractor commonly joins the project team by this phase.

VALUE ANALYSIS/VALUE ENGINEERING STUDIES

Value analysis/value engineering studies optimize value in project designs.

During design, the CM provides value analysis studies that consider the capital, operating, and maintenance costs to verify that the design achieves the most cost-effective lifecycle solution. If the team conducts the studies before developing the design data, the reports could be too conceptual. However, if the studies are delayed, then redesign may be necessary to reflect the study's recommendations.

NOTE: After construction begins, damages for lost profits may be awarded to the contractor if value engineering deducts work from the contract and the contract does not define this condition.

Value Engineering/Analysis

- ✓ Multi-disciplined, systematic, and proactive function to optimize value
- ✓ Least lifecycle cost, or provide the greatest value, while still meeting all functional, safety, quality, operability, maintainability, and durability goals established for the project
- ✓ Good for "designing to cost"
- ✓ About to go to construction
- ✓ During construction
- ✓ CM should take an active role

Therefore, it is best to complete these studies during the initial design development phase. The CM includes any needed independent experts such as a Certified Value Specialist (CVS).

COST MONITORING AND REPORTING

The CM provides any necessary ongoing cost monitoring to assist the designer with construction budget compliance.

In addition to cost reporting from estimates, the CM provides other cost reporting the owner might require. The CM should record all cost monitoring performed between the estimate submittal stages and forward these records to the owner as a part of the cost management system outlined in the Project Procedures Manual. The CM constantly monitors the design to identify scope changes, evaluate the time and cost impacts of those changes, and report the impacts to the project team.

When the CM and owner negotiate construction management services, they should determine the number of submitted estimates and the extent of ongoing cost management services, value analysis, tradeoff studies, and other similar activities.

3.4 Procurement Phase

ESTIMATES FOR ADDENDA

The CM fully prices all proposed addenda that have a cost impact. The quantification and pricing methodology should be consistent with the final construction cost estimate submitted for the owner's approval at the end of the design phase.

3.5 Construction Phase

The CM monitors cost management procedures throughout the construction phase and communicates cost and budget performance to stakeholders as appropriate.

SCHEDULE OF VALUES (SOV)

The project participants should review and agree to the SOV shortly after the contract award to avoid underpayments or overpayments during the project. If the SOV is not already part of the GMP proposal, the SOV's format is usually in the CSI division breakdown. The careful apportionment of indirect costs to the pay items ensures equitable reimbursement and avoids "front-end loading." For transparency, general conditions and overhead costs may be additional line items in the SOV.

The SOV should be detailed enough to allow accurate calculation of billed amounts but not add an unmanageable amount of detail. The SOV should reduce the occurrence of payment application disputes. There are two major methods for reviewing progress payments:

1. **Percentage of Completion of Scheduled Activities** – The CM and the contractor(s) determine the SOV for each of the scheduled activities which can be applied to a cost-loaded schedule for progress payments.

2. **Percentage of Completion by Division of Work** – The CM and the contractor(s) determine the SOV for each work element. This information should be the basis for all future progress payments to the contractor, as well as historical information for future project estimates.

CHANGE ORDER CONTROL

The CM develops and implements a change order control system for financial control during construction.

When participants agree that a change in the contracted scope has occurred which merits a change in contractor compensation, there should be an equitable adjustment to the contract price. To determine a fair adjustment amount, the CM reviews the supporting data as proof of costs. Legislation, contract requirements, or company policy often require organizations to provide an Independent Cost Estimate (ICE). The review process must have organized data and participants must thoroughly understand the change order's scope.

The CM prepares an estimate of the change order's cost that lists:

» The anticipated labor

» Material

» Equipment

» Subcontract work

» Contractor's overhead and profit

» Any justified impact costs

The CM should pay special attention to the scope of work reductions and analyze the change's time impact on the schedule. To avoid delays, the CM should complete this work before receiving the change order pricing from the contractor.

Two types of change order pricing may be involved:

1. **Forward pricing**: Pricing is done before or during the work. The estimate of costs should itemize production rates, crew compositions, hours, and equipment. This method lists material costs and substantiates them with quotes and price lists.

2. **Post pricing**: Pricing is done during or after the work and represents actual costs based on records of labor, material, and equipment. Comprehensive cost records are necessary. On force account work, the CM and contractor should both verify and document the work daily.

In forward pricing, the CM considers these special factors when evaluating production rates:

» Status and condition of the work

» Relative size and capability of the contractor(s)

» Size and complexity of the change

» Climatic conditions

» Mechanization that is possible

» Labor agreements

» Trade practices

» Learning curve

» Additional supervision required by the change

» Value of acceptance of risk

When evaluating material and equipment costs, the CM considers these special factors:

» Salvage of job material

» Odd lot sizes that add to cost

» Special delivery cost

» Potential higher price for proprietary items

» Escalation of costs since the original job was bid

» Storage costs that may be necessary

» Premiums for payment and performance bonds

» Potential for additional insurance coverage

» Additional inspection and testing costs

» Special equipment that may be required to perform the work

While impact costs, if any, may be difficult to quantify, the team should address the following issues:

» Changes in the sequence of work

» Changes in method and manner planned for doing the work

» Discontinuity of work

» Premium time incurred to overcome delays

» Congestion of work area/Trade stacking

» Added mobilization/demobilization (includes equipment, e.g., crane time)

» Impact on other work and other contractors

» Potential for rework

High impact costs, if any, can sometimes be determined by:

» Evaluating actual cost of identical work performed or what is sometimes referred to as a "measured mile" approach.

» A reasonable estimate of the work cost if a change had not been encountered compared to the estimated cost of change order job conditions or compared to the actual cost of work performed if using post pricing.

» Auditing the contractor's job cost records.

The original contract should establish allowed overhead and profit as fixed percentages on change order work.

TRADEOFF STUDIES

During construction, the CM performs component studies on materials, systems, equipment, and accessories to ensure that the team selects economical/competitive components consistent with the construction budget. The CM fully documents tradeoff studies and submits them along with the CM's recommendations to the owner and designer.

CLAIMS FOR COST

The CM establishes a detailed audit trail so that a complete record of all project-related financial transactions in order of activity is available in the event of subsequent audits, claims, or investigations. (See **Chapter 4: Time Management | Construction Phase**.)

3.6 Post-Construction Phase

The CM summarizes total project costs in a final report that lists all change orders and identifies any unresolved issues which may have a post-construction cost impact, such as a claim or other dispute. The CM should provide a summary narrative that includes assumptions on any post-construction cost impacts as well as a cost and change spreadsheet of final project accounting.

Notes

Notes

CHAPTER 4

Time Management

4.1 Introduction

Construction management involves the control of three basic project parameters: cost, time, and quality within the defined scope (including both the quantity and quality of the work). Construction management includes maintaining the proper balance among competing objectives.

All CMs recognize that these parameters are related and that a change in one can affect the others. In construction management, this linkage is sometimes called the "triple constraint" theory and is represented by a triangle with pinned corners. Increase or decrease the length of one side of the triangle and the lengths of the other sides change. If the scope increases, then the sides of the triangle representing cost, time, and quality may increase as well.

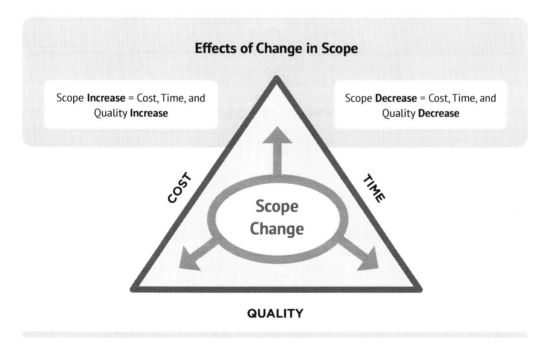

Effects of Change in Scope

Scope **Increase** = Cost, Time, and Quality **Increase**

Scope **Decrease** = Cost, Time, and Quality **Decrease**

COST

TIME

Scope Change

QUALITY

The CM's time management goals on a project are met when the CM makes the most effective use of people, equipment, materials, and funds to manage time. The CM achieves the most effective use of project resources through careful planning and expert execution.

The schedule is the CM's primary tool to meet these time management goals. Therefore, the preparation, use, and analysis of schedules define the time management standards in this section.

How the CM achieves these goals depends on project type, size, and complexity, as well as the constraints of time, cost, quality, and scope. Measuring a CM's performance must always consider the CM's role on the project, the applicable contract documents, and other project constraints.

Generally, the CM's time management responsibilities include:

» Ensuring that the project team develops a project plan to accomplish the project in an appropriate span of time.

» Ensuring that the project team develops a schedule to both plan and monitor the project's usage of time.

» Helping the project team select the best form and content for the project schedule.

» Leading the time management and scheduling effort.

This last responsibility has several pieces. Depending on the contractual relationships established among the parties on the project, the CM may be responsible for:

» Developing the project schedule, which may include everything from collecting the necessary work activity, duration, resource, and logic data, to assembling these pieces into a coherent plan for time on the project.

» Updating the project schedule regularly so the project team may track, measure, and monitor its progress against the original plan.

» Updating the project schedule so that it accurately defines the completion plan for the remaining project work.

» Revising the project schedule to reflect changes in the scope or plan of execution.

» Reviewing, recommending acceptance of, and monitoring the schedules, schedule updates, and revised schedules prepared and submitted by other project participants.

» Monitoring/analyzing the schedule to track the project's time performance and alerting other parties to deviations from the established plan.

» Recommending actions for the project team if the project falls behind schedule to bring the project back within established goals or recommending revisions to project goals.

» Preparing schedule analyses or reviewing, evaluating, negotiating, and making recommendations for time extensions or acceleration based on analyses other project participants prepare and submit.

» Advising the project team about contract provisions for scheduling and time extensions.

Notice that the words "accept," "accepted," and "acceptance" are used for consistency throughout this section in lieu of "approve," "approved," or "approval." Acceptance typically means that the party providing acceptance takes on the responsibilities associated with that acceptance as defined in applicable contract documents. If the contract documents are silent, then acceptance will generally mean that the schedule as submitted is deemed to follow the contract requirements and applicable industry standards.

Acceptance does not typically mean a guarantee that the work can be completed as scheduled, except for work that is the responsibility of the party conferring acceptance. For example, the owner's acceptance of the project schedule does not represent an endorsement of the contractor's plan or confer on the owner an obligation to ensure that the contractor can complete the work as scheduled. That obligation remains with the contractor. However, when the owner accepts a schedule the contract requirements may place an obligation on the owner to complete its scope of work as scheduled.

Importance of Time Management

- ✓ **Biggest Challenge**: deliver projects on time
- ✓ Time is not flexible
- ✓ Schedule issues lead to conflict
- ✓ Helps quantify time impacts
- ✓ Avoiding claims

The CM's time management approach varies depending on the stage of the project's development and execution. The following focuses on the Standards of Practice by project stage.

4.2 Pre-Design Phase

MASTER SCHEDULE

Typically, master schedule development begins with the CM and the owner agreeing on the time-related overall project goals. The CM will develop various approaches for phasing, sequencing, managing, and implementing the design, procurement, construction, and post-construction phases and discuss these alternatives with the owner.

Then the CM will prepare the project's master schedule based on the owner's instructions and submit it to the owner for acceptance. This schedule communicates the overall time-related goals in a format that the owner can understand.

The Critical Path

- ✓ The longest continuous path of project activities that controls the completion of the project
- ✓ On a new schedule the critical path has zero total float
- ✓ Delayed project total float is negative
- ✓ CPM schedule allows forecasting the effect of changes
- ✓ One day of delay to an activity on the critical path causes one day of delay to project completion

The schedule format may range from bar graphs or charts for small projects to Critical Path Method (CPM) networks for larger or more complex projects. The accepted master schedule may become an integral part of the PMP. (See **Chapter 2: Project Management | Pre-Design Phase**.)

After the owner accepts the master schedule, it is the CM's responsibility to monitor activity progress on the master schedule and to recommend or take appropriate action when progress deviates from the established plan.

ALTERNATIVE SCHEDULING

Scheduling is evolving with the construction industry. No longer satisfied with a "one size fits all" method, some professionals implement the *Last Planner® System of Production Control*[1] developed by the Lean Construction Institute.

In the *Last Planner®* workflow, the project team adds details to the baseline schedule over time. The baseline schedule does not begin with in-depth details, but it incorporates those details gradually throughout the project, as required.

Users who regularly implement *Last Planner®* report an increase in productivity and accountability through tight scheduling and detailed group planning.

MILESTONE SCHEDULE

After the owner accepts the master schedule, the CM may prepare a milestone schedule that highlights the master schedule's key events, particularly in the design phase. These dates might include the following:

» Design professional selection
» Completion of cost/benefit studies
» Completion of 30%, 60%, and 90% drawings
» Completion of design and constructability reviews
» Completion of bid packages
» Other potentially significant milestones

The milestone schedule may also include dates for other phases, such as the start and finish of procurement or construction. The milestone schedule should include critical dates that affect site availability as early as possible.

The milestone schedule may also include key intermediate milestones for the construction phase depending upon the requirements of the project. When the team manages programs consisting of individual but interrelated projects, milestone schedules establish the required time relationship between the projects.

FLOAT

The CM recommends specific provisions to handle float throughout the project for the owner's review and acceptance. The CM typically recommends that all parties to the contract share float until it is depleted. The CM recommends to the owner whether float should be determined relative to the scheduled completion dates or dates established in the contract. The CM also recommends how to address early completion schedules submitted on the project.

Once the owner accepts, the CM recommends how best to implement the owner's decisions to determine float, administer early completion schedules, and share float ownership. This may include recommending contract language and explaining this language to bidders.

EARNED VALUE

Earned Value Analysis (EVA) or Earned Value Management (EVM) is a set of procedures that may help assess a project's progress. It involves comparing the planned amount and cost of the completed work at a specific milestone with the amount of actual completed work and the actual costs. Below is an example of earned value calculations.

Earned Value Calculations

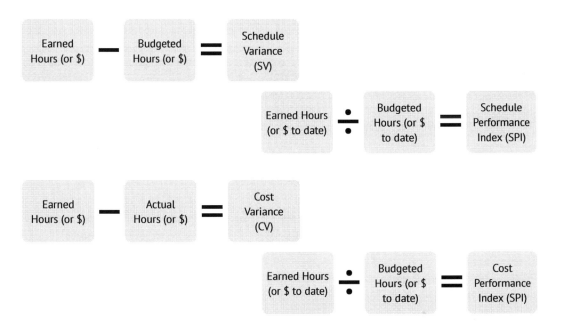

COST/RESOURCE-LOADED

A cost and resource-loaded schedule means that activities, along with their resources and estimated costs, have been scheduled throughout the project. Cost and resource-loaded schedules with EVA can help track resources and cost trends to monitor potential issues.

Cost and labor resources in resource-loaded schedules should stay current with the change work reflected as activities in the schedule.

If the schedule is cost or resource-loaded, or progress payments are made based on the schedule update, the scheduling provisions must agree with the contract's payment provisions.

SCHEDULING IN CONTRACTS

The owner may ask the CM to recommend specific scheduling and time extension requirements for the design professionals' contracts. This may include recommendations for the milestone schedule dates in these contracts. The owner may also ask the CM for scheduling suggestions for other contracts, such as the contractor's contract with the owner in agency CM.

On all projects, the contractor contracts should include a detailed schedule specification. This specification explains what the contractor must provide as an acceptable schedule.

4.3   Design Phase

MAINTAINING THE MASTER SCHEDULE

During the design phase, the CM monitors activities on the master schedule and updates the master schedule to reflect the project's design phase plan. The CM usually updates the master schedule monthly to reflect the actual progress on master schedule activities, but more frequent updates may be appropriate on short-duration, large, or accelerated projects. The design consultant or entity responsible for preparing the project design typically prepares the detailed design phase plan.

As the project's scope develops during this phase, the CM recommends revisions to the master schedule. Revisions may be the result of changes in the project scope, changes in regulatory or permitting requirements, site investigations, or design phase change orders the owner executes. For example, revisions may be necessary when the owner grants time extensions to the design consultant. As provided by the project contract documents, all affected parties should review and accept master schedule revisions.

The owner should receive all master schedule revisions for review and acceptance. Scheduling software helps facilitate collaboration and document scheduling changes if issues arise (e.g., missed deadlines).

DESIGN SCHEDULE

The designer or party responsible for preparing the project design typically works with the CM to prepare a realistic schedule for planning and executing the design phase. This schedule should be compatible with the master schedule, the milestone schedule, and the designer's contract requirements. After the owner accepts this schedule, the CM incorporates it into the master schedule and the milestone schedule.

Time Management in Design Phase

- ✓ Refine milestone schedule
- ✓ Define structure for program schedule
    - – Key players
    - – Key activities
    - – Identify long lead items; track in schedule
- ✓ Establish design milestones
    - – Example - 35%, 65%, 95%, and 100% design docs
    - – If Design-Build, establish review periods
- ✓ Refine durations of remaining phases

MONITORING THE DESIGN PHASE

The designer typically prepares monthly updates or revisions to the design plan and submits these to the CM for review. The CM uses these updates and revisions to monitor the progress of the project and identify any deviations from the established project plan. After review, the CM recommends appropriate actions to the owner. The CM usually recommends acceptance if the CM finds the schedule acceptable. After the owner accepts the proposed revisions, the CM revises the master and milestone schedules to reflect these revisions.

If the CM decides that the submitted schedule is deficient, the CM and designer typically work together to bring the submitted schedule into compliance with the master schedule, applicable contract provisions, and established industry standards.

If the submitted schedule shows the project ahead of schedule, the CM recommends how to bring the schedule into compliance with the project master and milestone schedules or recommends revisions to these schedules. This process may include the design professional reviewing requests for time extensions or acceleration.

PRE-BID CONSTRUCTION SCHEDULE

The CM may develop a pre-bid construction schedule and identify major milestones to include in the bidding documents before bidders receive them. The CM provides the pre-bid schedule information as a reasonable estimate of the proposed work sequence, contractual restraints, dependencies, and the contract or project duration. The CM's estimates are based on the completed design, the CM's experience, the project status, and other information available at bid time.

The bidding documents must also include other relevant information such as requirements, constraints, and detailed scheduling specifications. After the owner accepts the schedule, that information becomes part of each contractor's contract documents.

SCHEDULE REPORTS

The CM prepares and distributes schedule review and update reports to the owner and appropriate parties. These reports describe and graphically depict actual progress on the project during the design phase in comparison to the project plan shown in the accepted master, milestone, and design phase schedules. The reports should include a narrative describing progress, delays, schedule revisions, and recommendations to resolve time-related problems.

4.4 Procurement Phase

CONTRACTOR'S CONSTRUCTION SCHEDULE

At the pre-bid conference, the CM, owner, and design professional explain to bidders the project requirements in the scheduling specification. The CM explains the pre-bid construction schedule and the contractor's scheduling responsibilities. The objective is to define the contractor's responsibilities regarding schedule development and maintenance, cooperation, accountability, and compatibility with the contract documents' overall scheduling and reporting requirements.

The CM's objective is for the successful bidder(s) to become part of the project scheduling process. The CM provides a milestone schedule to the bidders and explains their scheduling responsibilities, including the obligation to participate in schedule development as required by the contract documents. The CM explains the contract document requirement for contractor(s) to prepare a construction schedule that includes the following:

» Applicable standards

» Requirements related to content and measurement of float

» Disposition of early completion schedules

» Float ownership

» Granting of time extensions

» Penalties or sanctions related to non-compliance with schedule requirements

In some contract formats, the CM produces and updates an overall schedule that incorporates information provided by each contractor or subcontractor. In other formats, the CM reviews the contractors' schedules and advises the owner on acceptance.

ADDENDA

Before issuance of the addenda, the CM reviews all addenda to determine the effect on scheduling and time of construction. The CM recommends to the owner any appropriate revisions to the master schedule and pre-bid construction schedule. After the owner accepts any revisions, the CM edits and distributes the revised schedules to the design professional and bidders.

SCHEDULE REPORTS

The CM prepares and distributes to the owner and other appropriate parties monthly reports that describe and graphically depict actual progress on the project relative to the project plan as shown in the accepted master, milestone, and procurement phase schedules (if prepared). The reports should include a narrative describing progress, delays, schedule revisions, and recommendations for actions necessary to resolve time-related problems.

Information to Update in the Master Level Schedule

- ✓ CM actions
- ✓ Designer actions / Design-Build firm actions
- ✓ Anticipated constructor start
- ✓ Commissioning
- ✓ Public notices, advertisement dates
- ✓ Complete bidding documents due date
- ✓ Request for Qualifications (RFQ), RFP date

- ✓ Anticipated time for addenda
- ✓ Bid due dates
- ✓ Award dates
- ✓ Notice to Award, Notice to Proceed (NTP), contract duration
- ✓ Substantial completion
- ✓ Beneficial Occupancy
- ✓ Punchout and Closeout milestones

4.5 Construction Phase

THE INITIAL OR PRELIMINARY SCHEDULE

A CM's responsibility is to ensure that a schedule is in place for each project phase and for each stage of each phase. At the beginning of the project's construction phase, a comprehensive, detailed project schedule may take several weeks to develop, depending on the scheduling method selected. Therefore, an initial or preliminary schedule can establish the contractor's first actions on the project and establish a tool to monitor the project's progress while the baseline project schedule is in development.

CMs must fulfill their obligations for the provision of an initial or preliminary schedule as these schedules become the tool for planning the earliest stages of construction, monitoring the contractor's initial efforts, and addressing any deviations from the anticipated plan. This includes evaluation of delays and determining entitlement to time extensions.

The CM ensures that the appropriate parties fulfill their contractual scheduling obligations and recommends appropriate actions if the parties fail to meet their obligations. This is true whether the CM is responsible for assembling and developing the schedule (such as with CMAR) or if the CM is responsible for managing and monitoring the schedules prepared by the contractor(s). Generally, CMARs develop the overall schedule used to monitor progress.

The preliminary schedule should include the elements in the pre-bid construction schedule and near-term information provided by the contractor(s) or subcontractor(s) performing the initial work. The CM defines scheduling parameters (such as when a phase of work might start or how long a particular trade has access to an area) but should reasonably balance the assumptions made by the parties performing the work regarding productivity, desired sequence, and overall timing of work. The schedule should represent a blend of these two extremes.

When a contractor is primarily responsible for scheduling and an agency CM is strictly in a review role, the CM's initial or preliminary schedule responsibilities are like their responsibilities throughout the project's construction phase:

1. The CM ensures that the construction contract requires the contractor to develop and submit an initial or preliminary schedule for acceptance before the start of construction. These requirements include identifying software or electronic submission requirements to ensure that the initial and preliminary schedule submissions are compatible with the master schedule software.

2. The CM monitors the contractor's performance and ensures that the contractor makes a timely submission of the initial or preliminary schedule.

3. If the contractor fails to submit the initial schedule as the contract requires, the CM informs the owner and makes recommendations to address the contractor's failure.

4. Upon the schedule's submission, the CM reviews the schedule to ensure compliance with the contract requirements. The CM either recommends acceptance to the owner or advises the owner on how to address the contractor's submission.

5. Once the owner accepts the schedule, the CM monitors the contractor's performance in relation to the initial schedule, notifies the owner of any deviations, and recommends to the owner how to address these deviations.

6. Approximately two weeks before the expiration of the initial or preliminary schedule, if the owner has not yet accepted the baseline schedule, then the CM recommends to the owner how to address the impending deadline. These recommendations could involve the contractor's submittal of an extension to the initial or preliminary schedule. This submittal should go through an evaluation process like the original submission of the initial or preliminary schedule.

THE BASELINE SCHEDULE

The CM plays a central role in the development, acceptance, implementation, and monitoring of the project's baseline schedule. Before construction, the CM is usually responsible for advising the owner on how to accomplish the project's scheduling and time management. During construction, the CM is then responsible for fulfilling its time management obligations as established in earlier phases.

As in earlier phases, the CM's responsibility will depend on its project role. The CM typically either develops the schedule based on its own plans and input from the contractors or subcontractors (such as when in an at-risk capacity) or reviews the schedule produced by the contractor(s) (typically when in an agency role).

For the baseline schedule, a CM's responsibilities include:

» Recommending appropriate actions regarding the contractor's time management and scheduling responsibilities in the contract.

» Monitoring the contractor's development of the baseline schedule and recommending to the owner actions to take when the contractor deviates from its scheduled performance.

» Reviewing the contractor's baseline schedule submissions to ensure compliance with the contract requirements and applicable industry standards as well as recommending to the owner actions regarding the contractor's submission. This should include:

- Acceptance or rejection of the schedule, an accompanying description of schedule deficiencies, and recommended corrections (where appropriate).

- Ensuring that the contractor considers all the parties involved with the project's execution so that the accepted baseline schedule becomes the plan for the project team, not just the contractor.

If the owner is self-performing a substantial amount of the work, is fast tracking the work with multiple contractors, or when construction is only a small piece of a much larger effort, the owner may want additional control of the schedule and be willing to accept the added responsibility (and risk exposure) of owning the schedule for greater involvement in determining the sequence and pace of the project. Under these conditions, the owner might delegate the responsibility to the CM to develop, update, and revise the project schedule.

On fast-track contracts with multiple-prime contractors joining at different times, an agency CM will often be best-positioned to develop the overall schedule, given its understanding of the overall sequence and the relationships among the various prime contractors' work activities.

However, the CM then assumes greater risk if its schedule does not prove viable or if work performance by one contractor affects the performance of others. The CM should clarify overall schedule objectives without unnecessarily dictating contractor means and methods. For example, it is crucial that the risk associated with applying the proper means and methods remains with the contractor.

SCHEDULE UPDATES

For effective time management, project participants must use the project schedule to plan and execute the work. The CM is responsible for monitoring actual events in relation to the dates and durations on the accepted schedule. Under some contracts, these responsibilities might also include schedule updating.

The CM uses the schedule on an ongoing basis to fulfill its obligations to monitor the performance of the other parties involved in the project's execution. The schedule must be current to remain a valuable planning and monitoring tool. This means that the CM recommends to the owner and then helps the owner implement a process to periodically update the project schedule. An updated schedule helps determine if progress is consistent with anticipated baseline schedule assumptions and is a tool for planning remaining work.

There is a difference between updating a schedule and revising it. For this discussion, "updates" are limited to incorporating actual performance information related to the schedule's activities. For example, updates may refer to adding the actual start and finish dates for activities and minor edits to the schedule's logic and durations. Revisions may be considered minor when they do not result in earlier or later scheduled completion dates for project milestones or do not appreciably affect the obligations of the various parties working on the project.

The CM's schedule update responsibilities are like those for the baseline schedule. For example, the CM generally produces the schedule update or reviews updates prepared by the construction contractor(s). However, the CM also compares the project's progress to the accepted schedule to ensure that schedule updates are accurate and to determine if actions are necessary to bring the project back on schedule.

The CM may also advise the owner of deviations from the accepted plan shown in the schedule update.

SCHEDULE REVISIONS OR REVISED SCHEDULES

Very few projects finish precisely as planned, so the project team often needs to revise the accepted schedule to maintain an accurate time management plan. These revisions reflect the project management team's decisions in response to project conditions. These decisions may require more than simple corrections of out-of-sequence logic or other small and insignificant adjustments to the schedule. The process of incorporating more substantial changes is typically known as revising the schedule.

The CM plays a crucial role when a revised schedule is necessary. The CM treats the situation similarly to the baseline schedule submission because of the potential impact on the owner's and other project stakeholders' decisions. If other parties do not recognize the need for revision first, the CM must recognize the need for project plan revisions and recommend to the owner how to address this need.

Once the project team recognizes the need to revise the plan, the CM's responsibilities are like those related to the initial schedule, baseline schedule, and schedule updates. In particular:

» If the CM is responsible for developing the schedule, it must incorporate input from the impacted contractors or subcontractors to develop the revised schedule.

» The CM informs the owner of progress on the revised schedule's development and makes recommendations when this process falters.

» The CM reviews all submissions to ensure contract compliance and recommends acceptance or rejection of these submissions to the owner.

» Upon acceptance, the CM shifts its focus to the revised schedule to monitor the project team's performance.

» The CM reviews the updated schedule to determine if it accurately defines the plan to complete the remaining project work.

If the contractor seeks a time extension at any point in the project, the CM ensures that the contractor submits time extension requests in accordance with the contract.

If possible, parties should negotiate and agree to time extensions before the associated delay occurs. This means that the CM must notice problems that might cause a delay before they occur. This happens most often when the owner considers a change and the project team has time to consider the change before proceeding. Regardless of the timing, the CM's responsibilities are similar. The CM:

» Ensures that the appropriate party conducts the necessary analysis to determine the magnitude of the delay and the party responsible.

» Reviews submitted time extension requests to ensure they are in accordance with the contract and correctly establish the time extension due, if any.

» Completes its review and recommends to the owner to accept the submission and execute an extension of time, acknowledge responsibility for the delay but consider acceleration to mitigate, or reject the submission with an appropriate basis.

» May seek additional time for itself (if CMAR), in which case it will need to present its basis and rationale to the owner in an appropriate manner.

The CM must maintain its role as defined by the project's contracts and not assume other parties' contractual roles or responsibilities. This ensures that the appropriate party fulfills its scheduling responsibilities and reduces the risk of the CM and owner taking over the contractors' planning and scheduling obligations.

MAINTAINING THE MASTER SCHEDULE

During the construction phase, the CM monitors activities on the master schedule. Master schedule updates reflect the detailed plan prepared for the project's construction phase. Master schedule updates also reflect the actual progress on master schedule activities and happen on a regular basis, usually no more often than monthly, though more frequent updates may be appropriate on short-duration, large, or accelerated projects.

Based on the detailed construction phase schedules, the CM recommends revisions to the master schedule. As stated in the project contract documents, all parties affected by the changes should review and accept the master schedule revisions. All master schedule revisions should be submitted to the owner for review and acceptance.

SCHEDULE REPORTS

The CM prepares and distributes to the owner and other appropriate parties reports that describe and graphically show actual progress on the project relative to the project plan as shown in the accepted master, milestone, and construction phase schedules. The reports should include a narrative describing progress, delays, schedule revisions, and recommendations for actions necessary to resolve time-related problems.

DELAY IMPACT

One of the CM's key responsibilities is to advise the owner regarding change order impacts on contract completion dates and other milestone dates.

Schedule impact analysis can help the owner understand the time implications of change orders or other anticipated owner actions or project events. Like change order cost estimates, schedule analyses can provide the owner with a forward-looking analysis of the estimated time impact due to change orders. They help the owner make a fully informed decision about whether to proceed with a change order. They also help focus the project team (including the owner) on potential actions to avoid or mitigate delays.

For more, see *CMAA Time Management Guidelines.*

4.6   Post-Construction Phase

OCCUPANCY PLAN

The CM may develop an occupancy plan that provides the owner with an orderly transition into the completed project and facilitates revenue income or beneficial use as quickly as possible. The occupancy plan should include the participation of contractors, system startup, completion of punchlists, city/state/federal reviews and certifications, and move-in of the owner's staff or tenants.

The CM submits its occupancy plan to the owner for the owner's review and acceptance. The CM incorporates the accepted occupancy plan into the master and milestone schedules for the project. Thereafter, the CM monitors the performance of work during the post-construction phase, updates the occupancy plan as appropriate, recommends corrective actions for any deviations from this plan, and provides appropriate reporting.

Post-Construction

- ✓ As-built schedule
- ✓ Review time impacts of change orders
- ✓ Occupancy/relocation schedules
- ✓ Follow on contract schedules
- ✓ Close-out schedules
- ✓ Transfer of title/ownership schedules
- ✓ Revenue forecasting schedules
- ✓ Facilities O&M schedules
- ✓ Commissioning
- ✓ Sustainability documents (LEED)

[1]*More information about the* Last Planner® System of Production Control *is available on the Lean Construction Institute website at* **https://www.leanconstruction.org.**

Notes

CHAPTER 5

Quality Management

5.1 Introduction

This section presents the key goals, philosophies, and elements of providing services while enhancing quality in the planning/design/construction process, the construction management services, and the constructed facilities.

QUALITY	QUALITY CONTROL	QUALITY ASSURANCE
A process that includes planning, organizing, implementing, monitoring, and documenting a system of management practices that coordinate and direct relevant project resources and activities to achieve quality in an efficient, reliable, and consistent manner.	The continuous review, certification, inspection, and testing of project components, including persons, systems, services, materials, documents, techniques, and workmanship, to determine whether or not such components conform to the plans, specifications, applicable standards, and project requirements.	The application of planned and systematic reviews that demonstrate that quality control practices are being effectively implemented.

Quality management is always part of the CM's basic service, regardless of the project delivery method or the level of effort required by the CM's contract. After an agency CM begins providing services, they should encourage the owner to develop and implement a comprehensive Quality Management Plan (QMP). This is one of the CM's first project tasks, no matter if the CM begins providing services during the pre-design phase, design phase, or after construction begins. This is also one of the first project tasks for a CM performing at-risk, whether the CM at-risk begins providing services during the pre-design phase or at the start of construction.

5.2 Pre-Design Phase

The goal during this phase is to establish a program of quality management that will endure throughout the life of the project.

CLARIFYING OWNER'S OBJECTIVES

The CM meets with the owner to clarify expectations and goals for the quality management program. It is important that the owner understand the underlying concepts of a quality process, quality services, and a quality project. The CM should review the value engineering strategy, including costs and benefits.

SCOPE OF WORK

The CM may review the design professional's scope of work to ensure that it clearly includes the proposed services that the owner accepted. The criteria to measure the completed project's success must be defined and clearly understood. This forms the basis for the QMP.

Consistent with CMAA guidelines, the CM reviews the design professional's contract for conformity with expected quality standards and related project criteria. This includes (but is not limited to) inspection/testing, sustainability, risk assessment, and commissioning. Before starting any work activity, the design professional should identify all quality-related design criteria and confirm that the owner accepts these criteria.

PROJECT ORGANIZATION

The quality management organization should include key representatives of the design professional, CM, and owner who are responsible for the implementation of quality control and assurance initiatives and preferably at the executive level.

QUALITY MANAGEMENT PLAN (QMP)

The CM develops a comprehensive project QMP with direct input from the design professional and the owner.

The QMP should identify the various steps in design development leading to approvals by the owner, users, government agencies, affected utility companies, and agencies having jurisdiction over the project. The plan should also provide for senior-level design professional review of design criteria, calculations, drawings, and specifications.

All parties should review and modify the QMP as required, then formally agree to the QMP. Subsequent revisions should undergo a formal modification procedure to maintain a current and effective plan.

5.3 Design Phase

The design phase goal is to implement the QMP to achieve a set of contract documents that support successful procurement and the project's completion in accordance with all the quality requirements.

DOCUMENT CONTROL

A document control system organizes, tracks, and distributes applicable documents during the project. The CM confirms that this system begins in the design phase and that it logs design progress submissions for each individual contract, with a tabulation of approved plans to be advertised. The document control system also applies to plans after bids are received, to conformed sets of plans illustrating all official addenda, and to change order plans during construction.

REVIEW OF DESIGN SUBMITTALS

The CM develops and implements a process so that all participants may review design submittals as they develop and verify that they achieve quality objectives. The CM documents and tracks the review/verification.

DESIGN CRITERIA CHANGES

When design criteria changes are directed or required and mutually accepted, the design professional should document them in a letter, email, or memo to the owner, with copies to the CM.

QUALITY CONTROL

The design professional should proceed with design activities that conform to the QMP. This process involves methods to check concepts, calculations, and material selection procedures to achieve the owner's quality expectations or the contract's quality requirements. Plans and specifications are reviewed for clarity, completeness, testing/documentation requirements, and consistency.

QUALITY ASSURANCE PLAN

The design professional should follow a quality assurance plan as part of the QMP. The quality assurance plan should include systematic reviews which demonstrate that quality control activities happened in an acceptable manner. Software that automates the routing and approval process may best achieve this.

A separate log should maintain the reports of items requiring corrective action for follow-up review and action before design completion.

The CM provides oversight review of the design professional's Quality Assurance (QA) efforts on the owner's behalf. All project stakeholders should collaborate to implement the QA plan effectively and efficiently.

MODELING

During the design phase, BIM or 3-D modeling may promote design coordination of various project elements, enhance quality, and reduce the necessity of rework for construction projects.

The CM may provide input on model details, such as the level of definition for the design elements and maintenance of the 2-D construction document that is printed during the procurement phase. If using BIM, the CM should ensure that there is a BIM plan that clearly documents the intent and associated responsibilities from start to finish. (See **Chapter 9: Technology Management**.)

CONSTRUCTABILITY REVIEWS

The CM develops and includes a specific constructability review program in the QMP. At a minimum, the constructability reviews should include a detailed review of the schedule, milestones, and constraints associated with the work, a field visit to confirm that the design considered existing conditions, and a detailed review of plans and specs to assure they are clear and coordinated.

Constructability reviews should happen at the 30%, 60%, 90%, and 100% completion stages of contract documents. Constructability reviews should also consider the availability of materials, availability and capabilities of local trades, and other local market conditions. The review should also confirm that the documents are suitable for bidding purposes.

SUSTAINABILITY

The CM should confirm that the owner has considered sustainability goals and objectives for the project. The project's sustainability expectations and the CM team's sustainability qualifications must be set as early as possible to align those expectations to roles and responsibilities among all project stakeholders.

When the QMP includes sustainability, the CM ensures that the owner established clear criteria for the sustainability scope of work, phases of implementation, team responsibilities, and expected outcomes and implications, be they fiscal, schedule, or otherwise.

VALUE ENGINEERING

The CM should discuss the costs and benefits of a formal value engineering analysis with the owner. If the owner agrees, the QMP should include provisions for a formal value engineering analysis at various stages of the work. A CVS should lead these reviews.

RISK MANAGEMENT

The CM confirms that the owner understands the benefits of a project risk management plan. When the QMP includes the risk management plan, the CM confirms implementation (including measurement and reporting to the owner).

ESTABLISHMENT OF CONSTRUCTION DURATION

The established construction duration has activity durations based on documented experience, historical data, or other recorded information, resulting in a pre-bid schedule in a CPM format.

CONSTRUCTION TESTING REQUIREMENTS

The contract documents should clearly identify the responsible party, testing requirements, and the acceptance criteria for all construction elements. The design professional should explain the specific tests that the owner expects the contractor, supplier, or owner itself will perform on-site or at the source (for example, a fabrication facility). Any material or product certifications which are required or are acceptable in lieu of tests should be noted.

QUALITY MANAGEMENT SPECIFICATIONS

The CM develops quality management specifications when acting as a CMAR or for the general contractor if acting as an agency CM. These specifications identify all parties' QA/Quality Control (QC) responsibilities, including organizational requirements for QA/QC.

On larger or more complicated projects, it is imperative that the CMAR or general contractor implements a written QMP. The plan identifies when the contract documents require quality management specifications. The CM confirms that the contract documents include these required specifications.

IMPLEMENTATION OF QA/QC REQUIREMENTS DURING CONSTRUCTION

The contract documents may include specific requirements for a CMAR or general contractor's QMP. The quality management specifications outline specific submission requirements for CMAR or general contractor QC activities and QA efforts. The CM ensures the implementation of the requirements. Performance of QC and QA activities can be a requirement for progress payments.

PUBLIC RELATIONS/USER REVIEW

The CM facilitates the end users' understanding of the design documents. Depending on the owner's organization, it is often appropriate for the project's end users to periodically review the design as it progresses. On public projects, the CM may help develop a task force of public representatives to review and discuss aspects of the project. On private projects, a task force of key personnel from the user group may consult while the design develops.

PROJECT FUNDING

The CM may verify that the necessary project funding is authorized and that all fiscal requirements are met (and will continue to be). This includes the allocation of appropriate funding for activities that specifically impact the project quality.

PROJECT REVIEW MEETINGS

Key project participants conduct project review meetings at least monthly, beginning in the project's design phase and continuing until completion of work. The meeting participants should review and discuss the design's QA and QC.

REPORTS

The QMP defines the reports required from the design professional during the design phase, such as foundation assessments, geotechnical reports, etc.

5.4 Procurement Phase

This phase's goal is to conduct the procurement process in a manner that will comply with all internal and external quality requirements as well as secure contractors and suppliers capable of satisfying those quality requirements. The result will be the successful and timely award of construction contracts.

PROCUREMENT PLANNING

The CM establishes the procurement phase's goals in the QMP. The CM should consult the master schedule, as outlined in Chapter 4: Time Management. The CM reviews the master schedule procurement cycle for advertisement, bid, and award together with any special approvals during the award cycle to ensure the schedule reflects market conditions and is reasonable.

ADVERTISEMENT AND SOLICITATION OF BIDS

The CM complies with prescribed standards for public agencies and private owners as well as proposes any modifications for consistency with the QMP. The CM participates in all pre-bid meetings, site visits, and addendum preparation.

SELECT BIDDERS LIST

Many owners use special lists to identify and prequalify bidders they believe are qualified to pursue work in their market. The CM helps the owner manage any prequalification steps or establish appropriate standards before any advertisements for bids.

Under a CMAR system, the CM must prepare a list of prequalified subcontractors and suppliers capable of performing the work.

INSTRUCTIONS TO BIDDERS

The CM ensures that the Instructions to Bidders section of a solicitation is comprehensive and includes clear, concise information that complements the advertisement or solicitation statement. Instructions should explain the procedures and requirements to submit an acceptable proposal for the owner's review.

PRE-BID CONFERENCE

The owner or the at-risk CM should hold a pre-bid conference for each contract that they solicit. The CM chairs this conference or supports the owner's PM in this task. Under CMAR, the CM runs the pre-bid conferences for all subcontractors and material suppliers. The CM introduces the bidders to the key participants that are present, including the owner, staff, design professional, and CM.

The CM reviews the relevant schedule information. This includes master schedule information if part of a multi-project program. Site visits are suggested, if not mandatory. The CM records the minutes of the pre-bid conference and site visit.

Bidders receive solicitation documents from the pre-bid meeting, so addenda must be issued for all direction that supplements or differs from these documents. This will maximize the likelihood of receiving quality bids.

PROPOSAL DOCUMENT PROTOCOL AND BID OPENING

Before and during the bid process, the team must control information about upcoming contracts in a manner that does not allow any bidder an unfair advantage over others. This may be accomplished manually or with a digital platform with controlled access.

The agency CM, design consultant, and owner use caution and good judgment to work together to maintain the "level playing field" required for uniform and fair bidding. In a typical public contracting setting, the owner and CM representative (if applicable) should open all bids received at bid opening and record the information, unless prohibited by statute.

The CMAR method may include opening the subcontractor and material supplier bids and compiling a summary of the results to review with the owner and design team, as applicable.

PRE-AWARD CONFERENCE

The owner and agency CM conduct a pre-award conference with the apparent successful bidder to review and discuss the terms, conditions, costs, and scope of work. The CMAR conducts similar pre-award conferences with the critical subcontractors. Regardless of the CM approach, using video conference software with recording capabilities is a best practice to document the conference session.

Depending on the issues involved, the conference could be a personal meeting with the parties or via telephone. The conference structure should ensure all parties clearly understand the contract and scope of work.

CONTRACT AWARD

The owner or CM formally notifies the successful bidder by letter that they are identified as the most responsive bidder for the contract or are otherwise selected to perform the work. The owner recognizes this letter as the Notice of Intent to Award. After receiving this notification, the CM advises the general contractor of the requirements to provide necessary bonding, insurance, and special requirements set forth in the instructions for bidders and contract documents.

Next, a Notice of Award is issued. The CMAR establishes contracts with all trade subcontractors and material suppliers that clearly define the bonding, insurance, and special requirements set forth in the instructions for bidders and contract documents. The subcontracts contain detailed scopes of work that supplement the contract documents in terms of construction means and methods.

5.5   Construction Phase

The following section focuses on the various quality initiatives that any project should incorporate in the construction phase and in the preparation of the detailed QMP for each specific project.

The goal of the construction phase is to complete construction in accordance with the contract documents' quality requirements, with documentation to verify the achievement of that compliance.

PRE-CONSTRUCTION CONFERENCE

The QMP should require a pre-construction conference that the general contractor or CMAR, owner, agency CM (when applicable), and design professional attend to review and discuss the overall project. This conference happens after the general contractor receives a Notice of Intent to Award but before the NTP.

The general contractor should present the general approach, including the project's QC, and introduce the contractor's key personnel to the owner's team. The exact process may be different under CMAR but will involve the CM setting QC procedures and plans for the project's execution.

NOTE: The Notice of Intent to Award, Notice to Award, and NTP need to be kept in the project record. Like all documentation, they should be discoverable and auditable.

CONSTRUCTION PLANNING AND SCHEDULING

The general contractor, CMAR, or agency CM (depending on how the contract is organized) that is planning the construction work effort must submit a detailed work schedule with identified quality hold points.

All parties may view this schedule as the performing contractor's anticipated plan for the work to be performed within the given construction time. The schedule submission should address construction milestones, as identified in the contract documents.

An agency CM typically reviews the schedule to verify it complies with contract requirements and may approve the schedule for use.

INSPECTION AND TESTING

Consistent with the QMP and the CM contract, the CM verifies (daily, if appropriate) that testing and inspection of the contractor's work take place to determine if the work is in accordance with the contract specifications. If the CM provides such services, the QMP provides for the quality control and assurance mechanisms to ensure the quality of the services.

A CMAR inspects all trade subcontractors' work daily to verify that it is performed in accordance with the contract documents and their detailed scope of work. The CM coordinates with all applicable third-party testing and inspection agents.

REPORTS AND RECORDKEEPING

An agency CM maintains thorough documentation of the project's daily inspection efforts.

In addition, records are maintained of all pertinent project data and correspondence, progress photos, and photos of existing conditions prior to the NTP. Correspondence would include all submissions by the contractor (with an agency CM) or subcontractors (under a CMAR contract), approvals by the owner, shop drawing submissions, logs, certifications, etc.

DOCUMENT CONTROL AND DISTRIBUTION

The CM establishes procedures for document control and distribution of approved contract plans and specifications. The CM issues all changed drawings, sketches, plans, etc., and maintains a log of all current documents to include redlines and as-builts. It is a best practice for the CM team to maintain a set of record documents and reconcile them as part of the pay application process.

NON-CONFORMING AND DEFICIENT WORK

The QMP states the specific requirements for quality control and QA. The general contractor and all trade subcontractor(s) should systematically review their own quality control efforts.

Periodically, some identified items are not in conformance with the contract specifications. The CMAR or general contractor must maintain a log of all such items until an acceptable action by the appropriate contractor or subcontractor moves them from active status to resolved or closed out. If applicable, the agency CM should receive all such logs. A best practice is to use automated technology for logging, routing, approval, and archive purposes.

PROGRESS PAYMENTS

With agency CM, the CM proposes an acceptable progress payment process to the owner (unless one already exists within the owner's existing plan of operations). The progress payment format should accurately represent all costs associated with the project, all current change orders, and contingencies. Under CMAR, the contract defines the progress payment process and may require a designated owner's representative to directly perform a review.

FINAL INSPECTION, DOCUMENTATION, AND PUNCHLIST WORK

Toward the end of the project or phase, the CMAR or general contractor may request a final inspection by specification requirements to determine if the work can be declared substantially complete.

Under an agency CM, if the CM believes the work is sufficiently complete, then the CM conducts the final inspection, which the contractor, designer, and owner attend. The CM also develops a punchlist of outstanding items. If all remaining punchlist items are inconsequential to beneficial occupancy, the contract may be declared substantially complete. After acceptable completion of all outstanding items, the contract may be accepted as complete. Under CMAR, the owner or design team may determine this.

COMMISSIONING (CX)

The commissioning authority (CxA) who is responsible for the delivery of the commissioning process should prepare and implement a formal commissioning plan. The plan identifies the equipment and systems to commission. Each item is tested under various levels of performance to demonstrate the capability to meet and sustain the system/equipment design. Issued reports document these activities.

The agency CM monitors commissioning to ensure implementation of the commissioning plan while the CMAR implements the commissioning plan.

BENEFICIAL OCCUPANCY/SUBSTANTIAL COMPLETION

The contract specifications should define beneficial occupancy and provisions for its use. Generally, it represents the time that the owner takes over a particular facility, structure, or area for use for its intended purpose. The agency CM assesses the quality of the facility, structure, or area to determine if it is acceptable for beneficial occupancy. Under CMAR, the owner or design team typically performs this assessment. The assessment may occur before all contracted work is complete.

The contract specifications should also define substantial completion. Generally, it represents the owner's recognition that the project is ready for occupancy or use in accordance with its intended purpose. Minor punchlist items which do not hamper the owner's use of the facility may be completed within a reasonable or specified date after substantial completion. The specified level of quality for accepted work elements should be achieved at substantial completion.

NOTE: This action begins the warranty and O&M period.

FINAL ACCEPTANCE

Final acceptance of the work generally requires the owner to issue a Certificate of Final Acceptance to the CMAR or general contractor for the work and to file a Notice of Completion. This states that the contract is completed with no outstanding items remaining. This is also the milestone by which the CMAR or general contractor will notify its bonding and insurance companies that no further obligations remain on the contract.

5.6 Post-Construction Phase

Achieving quality during the post-construction phase is largely a function of planning and preparatory actions in previous project phases, as well as expedient project closeout.

The QMP can require that the CM assist the owner in the review and implementation of O&M manuals associated with the installed equipment and assist in pre-warranty expiration date checkouts. Under CMAR, the CM prepares the O&M manuals and summarizes the pre-warranty expiration date checkouts.

QM ASSESSMENT WITH OWNER

After the project is complete and all CM services are nearly complete, the CM may review and discuss the project's overall quality management with the owner. A detailed discussion with the owner and key representatives is a best practice to objectively assess the project efforts and the received benefits. This allows all parties to build on the project experiences in a way that will enhance quality in future work.

FINAL REPORT AND RECOMMENDATIONS

The CM prepares a final report for the overall project with recommendations to the owner regarding work activities that may require re-evaluation for future work. The CM's contract should include these services, which the CM negotiated with the owner at the start of work.

Notes

Notes

CHAPTER 6

Contract Administration

6.1 Introduction

This chapter addresses the CM's administrative tasks during project execution and the administration and reporting requirements for all construction and consultant contracts. This chapter generally assumes that an agency CM is performing as the lead consultant on behalf of the owner. Where helpful, this section discusses elements specific to agency CM or CMAR separately. This chapter uses the term "designer" for consistency but, depending on the project, a design-build contractor or A/E (architect or engineer of record) may fill the role.

The stakeholders negotiate a construction contract which can include various documents that define the project details, such as delivery method, participant responsibilities, and risk management strategy. The CM acting as the owner's agent or representing the contractor as a CMAR may administer or manage the final contract agreement.

Contract administration includes managing the project to ensure timely completion within the budget and in conformance with the contract requirements. The CM establishes necessary systems, policies, and procedures to ensure adequate project controls are in place.

The CM must confirm that appropriate stakeholders are identified. It is also important to understand the basic responsibilities and interrelationships of all team members, i.e., the owner, the designer, the contractor, the CM, the consultants, and any required specialty professionals. Additionally, the CM must have functional knowledge of the relationships among management components such as time, cost, information, quality, safety, sustainability, and risk.

During the project, both the PMP and the Project Procedures Manual (PPM) must remain up to date with changes required due to various constraints such as budget, schedule, regulations, etc. These documents may require additional updates in later project phases as part of the CMP.

What are the benefits of documentation?	Why are documents/records needed?
✓ Conformance to the contract	✓ Organization
✓ Construction quality	✓ Project documentation
✓ Projection control	✓ Tracking and follow-up
✓ Problem solving	✓ Project continuity
✓ Dispute resolution	✓ Software user information
✓ Litigation risk management	

The CM may help establish the type of contract used for the project, but more often, the project delivery method and the owner's preference dictate selection. Each project requires evaluation, taking into consideration the project's unique conditions and requirements as well as local construction contracting practices. Larger, more established clients likely have standard contracts, while others may need CM assistance for recommendations to develop contracts tailored to their project.

CMs must review final contracts to ensure they include appropriate provisions for contract administration that conform to basic industry standards as well as the PMP and the PPM. CMs should stay informed of applicable contract contents, including changes, updates, and revisions.

The contract documents for a typical construction project consist of:

	SECTION	TITLE	CONTENTS
SPECIFICATIONS	Part I	Agreement	**Bid/Proposal Forms** ✓ Notice inviting bids/bid schedule ✓ Contractor certificates/list of subcontractors (public) ✓ Non-collusion/non-discrimination affidavits (public) **Agreement** ✓ Contract ✓ Licenses ✓ Workers comp certificate ✓ Performance/payment bonds
	Part II	Conditions (the boilerplate)	✓ Insurance ✓ Scope of work ✓ Change order processing ✓ Jobsite notice requirements ✓ Termination clause ✓ Dispute resolution procedures
	Part III	Technical Specifications	✓ Quality standards ✓ Acceptable materials and techniques ✓ Quality testing requirements ✓ Dispute resolution procedures
	Part IV	Drawings	✓ Drawings ✓ Blueprints

CONTRACT FORMATS

STANDARD FORMS	CUSTOMIZED OR COMBINATION FORMS
» American Institute of Architects (AIA) » ConsensusDocs » Design Build Institute of America (DBIA) » Engineers Joint Contract Documents Committee® (EJCDC®) » Owner-specific	» Federal, state, county governments » Education systems, colleges/universities » "Serial" builders

CM FOCUS

CM Agency Contracts	Architect Focus
✓ One or more construction contracts ✓ CM is the owner's principal agent ✓ The CM handles the contract administration ✓ The designer handles the design	✓ One or more construction contracts ✓ The designer is the owner's principal agent ✓ The designer handles the contract administration ✓ The designer handles the design

AT-RISK CONTRACTS

CM at-risk Focus	Architect Focus
✓ CM's extensive professional services during design ✓ Self-perform work only if low bid, owner approves, and a separate Guaranteed Maximum Price (GMP) contract is signed ✓ Owner may reject GMP, CM may continue as agent ✓ Owner may require additional services after GMP is signed	» CM's limited professional services during design » CMs may self-perform work at their own discretion without submitting bids » No option for owner to reject GMP and continue CM's services » No option for owner to require additional services after GMP is signed

CONTRACT MANAGEMENT

CMs must focus on a contract's components to ensure they are accurately represented and implemented throughout the project, including the following:

» Cost

» Quality

» Risk/Safety

» Sustainability

» Time

For more details, see the *CMAA Contract Administration Guidelines*.

6.2   Pre-Design Phase

To provide real value to the owner during the pre-design phase, the CM helps complete the project planning, initiates overall coordination among the project team members, and selects the designer.

PMP/CMP

The CM may work with the owner and other project team members to define and document the project requirements. The resulting document is known as the PMP, which typically outlines the plan and strategy to fulfill the project requirements after owner approval. The PMP establishes the project scope, budget, schedule, environmental conditions, basic systems to utilize, and the methods and procedures to follow.

Documentation for the project scope includes a combination of conceptual drawings, descriptive narratives, performance data, and budget information from the owner. After the team establishes the basic systems and procedures, they align them with the corresponding tasks in the PMP.

The PMP may also include the CMP. The CMP can be a component of the PMP or a stand-alone document/strategy that the PMP incorporates by reference. The CMP typically outlines the approach that will be used to manage the project's construction phase and identifies possible impacts on the area around the project. The CMP may also detail building schedules, costs, and the tasks to accomplish.

On projects with both a CM representing the owner and a CMAR, both would have to document project cost and time. The CMAR would typically handle the more detailed documentation. The CM representing the owner would use the documentation to manage time issues during the project.

PROJECT PROCEDURES MANUAL

The CM should develop a PPM that clearly defines the project team's responsibilities, levels of authority, and the systems, methods, and procedures for project execution.

PROJECT DELIVERY

Even before design, the CM should advise the owner about the available project delivery methods, e.g., design-bid-build, design-build, multiple-prime contracting, CM at-risk, and others. The CM's analysis should consider which option best satisfies the owner's project objectives. Several factors significantly influence the amount of outside assistance required during the process and may guide the owner to determine the appropriate project delivery method, including the owner's familiarity with the construction process, the level of in-house management capability, and the degree to which the owner's standards or requirements dictate the final design.

An owner must assess its ability to properly administer each type of delivery method. The selected delivery method significantly impacts the project team member organization, roles and responsibilities, project risk, and the project's contract administration procedures.

MANAGEMENT INFORMATION SYSTEM (MIS)

During this phase, the CM should also establish the MIS that will inform the project team of the project's overall status and forecast compared to the established PMP. The MIS should address the team's information needs, data sources, elements for time and cost control functions, and output measures, as well as explain how to organize and implement the system. It should provide a sound basis to manage the project as well as identify and evaluate problem areas and variances. This requires tailoring a comprehensive system to the specific project.

To satisfy the need for a system that is simple to use, easy to understand, and capable of efficiently handling many common tasks, the CM should consider using an automated MIS. While not essential, a computerized MIS enables the CM to track, monitor, and organize thousands of items with a minimum investment of staff time.

A computerized MIS is most effective when all project stakeholders have individual access to the documents that pertain to them. The disadvantage is that cloud-based information systems with this capability may be expensive and cost-effective only on larger projects or for serial builders.

A CM may choose to invest in a subscription to an industry-standard cloud-based MIS and provide accounts to stakeholders, compensable as part of the service they offer to the owner. This also allows the CM to effectively extract critical historical data from completed projects, which better informs the estimation, scheduling, and planning of future projects.

An effective MIS also provides robust document management capabilities, including storage of design data. The CM can use the MIS to manage costs, administer contracts, and access documents and change orders instantly using mobile devices, which is especially important when on-site. (See **Chapter 9: Technology Management**.)

The CM should interview the owner's and the designer's staff personnel and determine the type, format, and frequency of information and reports required. At a minimum, information should include schedule and progress reporting, drawing schedules, budget versus cost of services, and change requests (approved and pending) for design services. The MIS should issue the first reports during the design phase and thereafter, on an agreed frequency.

Tools for tracking project details include:

» Document log	» Change order log
» Submittal log	» RFI log
» Material status report	» Issues book
» Follow-up list	» Reports

SUSTAINABILITY PLAN

The CM helps the owner establish the sustainability plan's goals and objectives, which the Owner's Project Requirements (OPR) may capture. Meeting the owner's time, cost, quality, sustainability, and other performance requirements may require many conceptual design and estimation iterations. Once the owner approves these requirements, the team must commit themselves to complete the project within those requirements.

OWNER'S PROJECT REQUIREMENTS (OPR) DOCUMENT

The CM may work with the owner to develop an OPR. This document provides an overview of the project and specific guidance to the design team with a focus on project performance and expectations. During the OPR's development, the CM can advise the owner on the cost and schedule impact of these goals so the owner can make informed decisions and goal tradeoffs before the project's design.

The project owner prepares the OPR to convey the project's functional requirements and the expectations of the project's use and operation. The OPR should address the following minimum issues as applicable to the project:

» Owner and User Requirements

» Technical Requirements and Standards of Construction

» Environmental and Sustainability Goals

» Energy Efficiency Goals

» Indoor Environmental Quality Requirements

» Equipment and System Expectations

» Building Occupant and O&M Personnel

CONCEPTUAL STUDIES

The CM prepares initial cost estimates and construction schedules to assist the owner or designer with preliminary feasibility and design studies. The CM may also recommend construction materials and methods that are best suited to the proposed project, common to the project (and its location), or feasible alternatives that meet the project's sustainability goals. The CM may assist the owner's evaluation of preliminary design alternatives and value engineering study.

PRE-DESIGN COST INVESTIGATION

The CM establishes a cost management plan, which becomes the basis and framework to control the project's costs. The CM provides cost estimating support for project feasibility and energy conservation studies as well as conceptual budgeting. The CM develops cost models to identify all project costs, including probable costs of construction, site acquisition, permits, consultants, escalation, and financing.

After establishing the project's master budget, preliminary cash flow and funding studies should be performed, including the approval of the release of any contingency funds.

MASTER SCHEDULE

The master schedule provides details about the front-end activities of the project during the pre-design and design phases. It also highlights major project milestones such as substantial and final completion.

The CM develops the master schedule to govern the life of the project. The CM establishes the overall schedule completion goals of future phases, including construction and post-construction. The CM also considers the budget because the duration of the overall project (and the duration of each phase) significantly impacts project cost.

MILESTONE SCHEDULE

The milestone schedule acts as a "pull out" from the master schedule. The milestone schedule's purpose is to highlight a project's key events as an executive-level summary.

The milestone schedule helps the project team realize the "big picture" because it consists of detailed activities (especially those related to pre-design) and identifies the key milestone activities and critical dates for their completion. The CM establishes the milestone schedule and monitors it with each update of the master schedule to keep the project team aware of critical time elements and their status throughout the project.

DESIGN CONSULTANT SELECTION

One advantage of selecting a CM early in the project (or having a CM on staff) is that if the chosen delivery method requires a separate design contract, the CM may help the owner select a designer. This includes developing Statements of Qualifications (SOQ), Requests for Proposals (RFP), and criteria to evaluate the proposals.

DESIGN CONSULTANT CONTRACT

If the owner requests it, the CM helps the owner prepare the designer's contract. The CM ensures that the contract scope of work is clear and complete and that the deliverables' submittal requirements are explicit. The contract must define and carefully coordinate the designer's specific responsibilities to prevent overlap with the owner and CM's responsibilities.

6.3   Design Phase

This phase's goal is to produce a complete set of contract documents that define a project and are deliverable in the current local market within the owner's established budget, performance, time, and quality requirements. In many ways, the design phase is the most critical project phase because it establishes the project's financial, legal, sustainability, and quality-based criteria. Good design documents and appropriate action in the design phase can avoid many of the obstacles that surface during construction and post-construction.

ADMINISTRATION AND COORDINATION OF DESIGN CONTRACTS

The CM reviews the contracts (including the scopes of work) to fully understand the requirements for each designer and sub-consultant. The CM's role is primarily coordination and guidance to help the owner in its contract administration of the schedule. The CM also conducts meetings to communicate all available project information (including the owner's desired features) to the designer to facilitate the design process.

The CM must have a working knowledge of the design practice and the standard procedures of a design firm, including deliverables, scheduling requirements, and productivity capacity. The CM may also be responsible for modifying the design contract with input from legal counsel.

MASTER SCHEDULE

Once the design scope of work is finalized and the design firm(s) submit the final design schedule, the CM amends the master schedule to include a detailed design schedule. The master schedule should have design, review, agency approvals, and permitting milestones. This should include:

» Schematic design, review periods, and cost estimate preparation.
» Value engineering, sustainability, and constructability reviews.
» Design development, review period, and cost estimate preparation.

- » Commissioning reviews of design development and construction document phases.

- » Agency approvals, time, and funding authorization milestones.

- » Review of design documents to ensure the design documents include OPR goals.

- » Completion of the Basis of Design (BOD) document by the design team.

- » Construction document completion, with approval time at the appropriate percentage of completion, accompanied by review periods and cost estimate preparation.

DESIGN PHASE COMMUNICATION

The CM develops and implements a system to expedite and control the flow of information during the design phase. Effective communications will enhance productivity, hasten design completion, expedite problem resolution, and minimize unexpected events or surprises.

QUALITY MANAGEMENT SYSTEM (QMS)

During the design phase, the CM should determine the specific approach to achieve quality in the design documentation. The agency CM should ensure that the contractors' and subcontractors' QMS meets the owner's QMS requirements. The agency CM confirms that the design quality management activities happen at the appropriate level to address quality control and QA.

DESIGN REVIEWS

The CM schedules design reviews and contributes to these reviews to help minimize design changes. These reviews prevent some problems, including unreasonable delivery schedules, confusion over responsibilities, unreasonable quality expectations, and improperly investigated conditions. These problems usually show themselves with an added cost to the project in short-term and lifecycle terms, as well as schedule slippage which increases project cost.

SUSTAINABILITY REVIEWS

The owner, architect, and CM should agree on the detailed scope and number of sustainability reviews required in design based on the requirements and goals set at the project's initial stage. Sustainable design seeks to reduce negative impacts on the environment and promote the health and comfort of building occupants, thereby improving building performance. Sustainability's basic objectives are to reduce consumption of non-renewable resources, minimize waste, and create healthy, productive environments while preserving resources for the needs of future generations.

CONSTRUCTION CONTRACT SPECIFICATIONS AND DRAWINGS

Drawings define a project's geometry (including dimensions, form, and details), whereas specifications define the project's qualitative requirements, such as the materials to be used, the construction procedures, and the workmanship expectations. Specifications also explain the project administration requirements during construction.

Construction specifications provide guidance on the contract's full requirements because they incorporate various standards, codes, and other publications. The project team should create the specifications early in the project lifecycle to establish performance requirements at the project's beginning and reduce overall risk.

The Construction Specifications Institute (CSI) published one of the first standards to consistently organize specifications between projects. CSI's MasterFormat® is now one of the most popular standards in the United States and Canada. The specifications information contained in MasterFormat® is organized in a standardized outline format with 50 divisions (there were 16 divisions until 2004).

Other common specification formats include National Master Specification (NMS) for projects in Canada and Unified Facilities Guide Specifications (UFGS). United States Department of Defense and NASA construction projects require design teams to use UFGS.

It is a significant investment for any organization to adopt a new specification format standard or update a specification system. The prudent CM will define the specification standard that best fits the project's requirements and is familiar to the project stakeholders.

TECHNICAL SPECIFICATION REVIEWS

The CM uses the project team's expertise to review the specifications for accuracy, clarity, and intent. This helps the contractor determine the full project requirements.

The review should check the reference specifications and the owner's standards for applicability, consistency, and clarity. The review should also compare the project specifications to the requirements of local jurisdictions, whose requirements may ultimately be the standard of acceptance. If using "or equal" procurement provisions, ensure that criteria against which alternates are to be evaluated are clear and complete. Clarify if bidders must prequalify alternates during the bid period or during construction.

SCHEDULING SPECIFICATIONS

The CM should prepare the scheduling specifications based on the complexity of the project in terms of the level of detail and the software required. The CM may also wish to consider the scheduling capability of likely contractors for the project.

The CM should prepare the specification section on scheduling and establish milestone dates with any appropriate constraints placed upon the sequence of the work or duration of key activities. The scheduling provisions must discuss preparation and acceptance of the contractor's schedule, as well as responsibility and procedures for updating the schedule. If the schedule is resource-loaded and progress payments are made based on the schedule update, the scheduling provisions must agree with the payment provisions of the contract.

Most scheduling specifications will require the contractor to create a CPM schedule or Gantt chart using computer software. (See *CMAA Time Management Guidelines*.)

However, the CM should recognize that owners increasingly ask contractors to apply lean construction principles, methods, and practices. **The CM must understand that many traditional scheduling specifications contain requirements that do not support lean project planning and execution.**

Many contractors adopt the construction activity planning and execution principles in the *Last Planner®* *System of Production Control* from the Lean Construction Institute. *Last Planner®* is a production planning system that involves the actual trade supervisors preparing a milestone project baseline schedule, which the team populates with detailed activities on an ongoing basis.

CONSTRUCTABILITY REVIEWS

Project designs too often do not fully consider the cost or difficulty of construction, so to contribute major value, the CM and the contractor review the contract documents from a constructability, maintainability, and claims avoidance perspective. Implementation can include varying levels of effort ranging from simple drawing and specification reviews to site visits (to ensure spatial accuracy).

This process should also place special attention on the dependencies or logical relationships between construction tasks as the schedule develops. This ensures that the schedule reflects the reality of construction operations and accurately describes what will happen when construction begins.

Based on the outcome of the contract documents review, the CM may recommend alternative construction and contractual methods and procedures to the owner if they benefit the overall project schedule and budget. The CM strives to minimize potential change orders and claims throughout the construction phase.

COMMISSIONING REVIEWS

The commissioning agent (CA) is an independent, third-party consultant who is directly accountable to the owner. The CA is responsible for developing and coordinating the Commissioning Plan's execution. During the design phase, the CA must confirm that design documents (plans, specifications, BOD, etc.) are consistent with each other, include commissioning requirements, and meet the OPR.

The commissioning reviews verify that the commissioning process meets the OPR and BOD. In particular, the reviews confirm that there are adequate access points, test ports, monitoring capabilities, and control features. Reviews also verify that energy efficiency, operation, control sequences, maintenance, training, and O&M documentation requirements are consistent with the OPR and BOD.

DESIGN PHASE PROGRESS

During the design phase, the CM develops and implements a system for information regarding design progress to flow to all project team members. The CM informs the team of any actual or potential constraints to the project goals and recommends corrective action in writing. The CM also maintains a review and consultation process among team members on all relevant issues.

VALUE ENGINEERING

The CM arranges and participates in a value engineering (VE) review for the project. VE's goal is to obtain the best overall value for the life of the project and its intended uses while finding opportunities to substitute less expensive, more constructible, or more available materials that do not compromise function.

A multi-disciplined team that can bring the full and balanced perspective of all disciplines performs the best for a VE review. The VE team should identify features that do not contribute to quality, utility, durability, aesthetics, or other specific owner requirements. The VE process must carefully consider and not compromise the project's sustainability objectives.

CONSTRUCTION CONTRACT PACKAGING

The CM helps the owner develop an overall procurement strategy for the project. This plan considers factors such as local practices, the local labor market, chances of unfavorable site conditions, etc., to evaluate the use of a general contractor, multiple-prime contractors, design-build, or other delivery methods, as well as the use of phased construction.

The CM also helps the designer and recommends and prepares the contract documents required to implement the procurement plan. The owner and legal counsel should review all such documents before use. This includes:

» Instructions to Bidders

» Bid Form

» Standard Bond Forms

» Form of Agreement

» General Conditions

» Detailed Scope of Work

» Supplemental Conditions

Finally, the CM should review the proposed owner/contractor agreement for common pitfalls, such as:

» Poorly defined scope of work, gaps in scope, or duplication between contracts.

» Failure to define allowable mark-ups for the general contractor and subcontractors/sub-subcontractors, as well as the mark-ups on deductive changes.

» Unrealistic schedule or phasing provisions.

» Lack of damages clauses for missed milestone completions.

» Lack of method to deal with unforeseen conditions.

» Lack of establishing contingent or alternative bid items.

» Unclear sustainability goals and unclear responsibilities to meet these goals.

» Assigning permit responsibility inappropriately.

» Unclear evaluation criteria to determine low bidder. (Are unit prices, alternatives, and VE included in the evaluation of base bid?)

» Unclear bonding and insurance requirements.

CONSTRUCTION PHASE BUDGET

The CM should prepare detailed cost estimates as information becomes available during the design phase. These detailed cost estimates prepared during the design phase will constitute the final project construction budget, against which actual construction costs will be monitored.

Early in design, before establishing the specification sections, the CM must develop cost models using other formats. It is critical to establish the relationship of scope, quality, and time to cost. By linking a functional program to project elements, it is possible to develop a model to track scope and cost through the design process.

After developing CSI specification sections, standard off-the-shelf computer models can accurately track project cost if the SOV is accurate with the correct specification taxonomy. As each design phase finishes, the CM updates the cost model, including changes in previously estimated costs, and holds a meeting with the project team to review the status and adjust, as necessary.

PRE-BID CONSTRUCTION PHASE SCHEDULE

The CM develops a guide in the form of stipulated milestones or a preliminary construction schedule to include in the construction bid packages. The pre-bid schedule serves as a basis to record information used to estimate the overall construction time. The pre-bid schedule should indicate any special assumptions made regarding shift work or extended hours.

ADDITIONAL PROJECT-SPECIFIC TASKS

CM services vary according to project type and many of these services fall outside the traditional scope of construction services. For example, in the renovation of an occupied building, the CM may help negotiate, plan, and implement a swing space; plan temporary protection measures for the public or occupants; organize and conduct informational meetings to discuss disruptions to building operations; keep phone and computer service uninterrupted; and develop an office furniture relocation plan. The CM will also help develop and implement an indoor air quality plan to minimize the transmission of odors and dust from construction into occupied spaces.

6.4 Procurement Phase

Procurement of professional and construction services will generally happen in one of three ways:

1. Priced based

2. Qualifications based

3. Best value (combination of 1 and 2)

Procurements may also involve a one-step process with a single round of submittals that determine the selection, or a two-step process which may include a qualifications submittal as the first step and then a price proposal as the second step. The CM might also consider a sole source/non-competitive approach when seeking specialty services that are not a commodity and include documentation to support the recommendation.

In a design-bid-build project delivery process, the procurement phase for the construction contractor typically bridges the time between the design completion and the start of construction. However, the timing of contractor procurement will match the project delivery method the owner selected. (See description in **Chapter 2**.)

For D-B, the contractor is part of the team the owner selected before design. For CMAR (CM/GC), the owner typically selects the contractor just after the design starts. (For a project in the public sector, a purchasing agent may handle procurement until the bid is tabulated.)

DEVELOPMENT OF BIDDERS LIST

Project bidding may be open to all interested bidders or only open to prequalified bidders, depending on the owner's requirements and government restrictions. The CM helps the owner develop a list of potential bidders from any of the following categories:

1. Contractors successfully employed by the owner in the past

2. Contractors that either the CM or designer recommend

3. Contractors known to be looking for work and that possess the necessary expertise and capacity to perform the work

BIDDERS INTEREST CAMPAIGN

For a selected bid list, the CM conducts a telephone/written campaign to generate maximum interest among qualified contractors. This includes contacting local and regional builders found in the telephone listings/internet search, referred by local designers, involved in construction or trade associations and bidding exchanges, etc. The CM should formally record information received from the bidders and present it with other data used to determine the bidders list.

BIDDERS PREQUALIFICATION

If possible, the CM should develop a contract scope breakdown for each trade contract on the project. The breakdown should consider the availability of design information, schedule, and local contracting practices. Along with the scope development, schedule information should be produced that includes key dates for receiving technical information, reviews and approvals, bidding, evaluation, and contract award.

BID ADVERTISEMENT

In the public bid process, the CM helps the owner prepare and place notices. Government agencies usually have a prescribed method for contacting vendors and contractors. The process must adhere to all legal requirements. When the owner does not dictate the method of advertising the bid, the CM must develop a program to attract qualified contractors.

The notice should be clear regarding scope, schedule, bonding, pre-qualifications, and any special owner requirements. Notices are usually placed in newspapers, trade publications, bid services, etc., in the project's geographic region. Contractors who have expressed interest should be contacted directly.

DISTRIBUTION OF BIDDING DOCUMENTS

The CM should coordinate with the designer to establish specific procedures that control the distribution of bid documents. This includes determining if documents will be distributed for free, for a charge, or for a deposit. Unsuccessful bidders normally receive deposit refunds upon return of the documents in good condition. It is important to ensure that enough copies of the bid documents are available for distribution.

ADDENDA

After the bid documents' distribution, all plan holders should receive addenda for any new clarifications and changes. During the bid period, the CM monitors the designer's preparation of addenda and controls their distribution. Addenda should be numbered and dated for easy reference as well as mailed to all plan holders of record, often via certified mail to assure receipt.

PRE-BID CONFERENCE

The pre-bid conference gives bidders an opportunity to become familiar with the project site and surrounding areas. To this end, the pre-bid conference agenda should include a guided site tour. The conference provides an opportunity to review the project, emphasize aspects of the project, review the project's sustainability goals, and discuss schedule milestones, as well as review staging areas, access, security, permits, and special safety requirements.

The CM should conduct the pre-bid conference, take minutes, and coordinate the responses to questions with the owner and designer. Based on the site conditions or the complexity of the work, the CM determines if a site visit is mandatory for all prospective bidders. The solicitation should include notice of the prebid conference.

INFORMATION TO BIDDERS

The CM establishes the procedures that set deadlines for bidders' questions, coordinates responses to questions, and distributes the answers to plan holders. All questions should be directed to a single contact within the CM's organization to be kept for future reference. The CM documents all inquiries and responses.

BID OPENING AND EVALUATION

The CM helps the owner receive and record bids at the formal bid opening and thoroughly evaluates all information in the bid. Most public agencies and many large private owners have specific procedures for bid document protocol and bid openings. The CM must understand these and instruct project team members accordingly.

PROCUREMENT OPTIONS

For the procurement of construction services, the chart below illustrates the use of the various options.

Selection Criteria	Low Bidder	Best Value	Best Qualifications
Project Delivery Method	Selection is based solely on price	Selection is based on a weighted combination of Price and qualifications	Selection is based solely on qualifications
Design-Bid-Build	Most Common	Common, price evaluation based on construction cost	Rare
Construction Management at-risk	Rare	Most Common; Price evaluation based on CMAR Fees and General Conditions	Common
Design-Build	Common	Most common, price evaluation based on CMAR fees and general conditions	Common
Integrated Project Delivery	Rare	Common	Most Common

A single procurement will procure services for a single project or for multiple projects.

By far, the most common procurement method is the single project award. In this method, an owner has a specific project and they only procure services specifically for that project.

The other procurement option is the multiple project award method, of which there are several variations. This method applies to the procurement of both professional services and construction services. With this method, an owner procures the services of one or more firms to perform a series of projects which are also sometimes known as tasks. Each project is priced separately, but all projects use a single contract vehicle.

The various types of multiple project (task) awards include:

» Indefinite Delivery / Indefinite Quantity (IDIQ)
» Multiple Award Task Order Contract (MATOC)
» Single Award Task Order Contract (SATOC)
» Job Order Contracts (JOC)

PRE-AWARD CONFERENCE

The CM reviews the project with the recommended successful bidder before the contract signing to ensure that there is a clear understanding of the project scope. The CM should review the project's technical requirements with the contractor and confirm either the absence of any bid errors or the existence of any errors and omissions in the contract documents. The CM should review the sustainability goals with the contractor and confirm they understand their role in obtaining these goals.

After finishing this review and validating the contractor's bid, the Notice of Award formalizes the relationship and begins the preparations for construction. The Project Manual is finalized, subcontractors are selected (if they are not already), and other tasks are accomplished to ready all stakeholders for the project's construction phase.

NOTICE TO PROCEED (NTP)

Once the parties are satisfied and execute the contract, the CM prepares the NTP for the owner and issues it to the contractor. The NTP establishes the construction contract start date and authorizes the contractor to proceed with the work. Often, a purchase order to which the contractor makes pay applications accompanies the NTP.

SCHEDULE MAINTENANCE

After the selection of the contractor(s), the CM should update and revise the project master schedule as necessary with information gained from the bid process. This includes updating the actual dates for receipt of bids, award of contract, NTP, etc. The CM should also revise schedule logic, activity durations, etc., to reflect the contractor(s) work plan. The CM then distributes an updated project schedule report that explains the effects of this information on the overall project.

COST REPORTING

The CM should update the cost report to compare actual bid prices to the budget figures. This may include updating the cost elements in a cost-loaded, computerized project master schedule and preparing the appropriate cash flow projections.

6.5   Construction Phase

All the planning and organizational efforts during the pre-construction phases help to successfully implement the PMP during the construction phase. The goal is to expedite and improve the construction process's efficiency through professional planning and execution of project activities, with a focus on fulfilling the owner's scope, cost, quality, and time requirements.

PRE-CONSTRUCTION CONFERENCE/MEETING

The CM should chair a meeting of all key project participants as soon as possible after the award of the construction contracts. The purpose of this pre-construction conference is to introduce the key team members to each other, familiarize all concerned with the various administrative requirements of the project, and ensure that each participant understands the requirements to fulfill their contracts.

At a minimum, attendees at this meeting should include:

» The owner or its authorized representative(s).

» Key members of the CM's staff.

» Representatives from the designer and its principal sub-consultants.

» The general contractor or each prime contractor, including executives, PM, and project superintendent(s), as appropriate.

» Major subcontractors, represented by their project managers or superintendents, as appropriate.

» The commissioning agent.

» The sustainability consultant.

» Representatives of relevant public agencies, utilities, or regulatory authorities.

» Any important material or equipment suppliers.

The CM should review the project's sustainability goals with the contractor and their subcontractors to confirm they understand their roles to complete these goals. The commissioning agent should attend the meeting and review the project's commissioning requirements. (See *CMAA Sustainability Guidelines*.)

Each project is unique, but there are certain concerns and issues common to all types of construction. A typical pre-construction conference includes an introduction of key project personnel that establishes everyone's role, responsibility, and authority. This includes a review of the relationships and responsibilities of the owner, CM, and designer. The review should also include communication protocols, document distribution, and decision authority (with clarifications if necessary).

The pre-construction conference also provides an opportunity to review completion issues to help avoid surprises at the project's end. This includes defining substantial completion and procedures for completing the punchlist items. The discussion should also include warranty requirements and procedures for "callbacks." Finally, the review should include contract closeout requirements, such as record drawings, O&M manuals, commissioning documentation, owner training requirements, lien releases, and final payment.

CONTRACT AND SPECIFICATION REQUIREMENTS

After contract award, the first administrative task is to review the contractor's, the CM's, and the owner's requirements and specific obligations. The contract sets forth these requirements and obligations, largely in the specifications, contract clauses, special clauses, and applicable industry standards.

CONSTRUCTION MANAGEMENT PLAN (CMP)

Updates to the CMP and PPM made at this stage should include the contractor(s) and any other new project team members, as well as any changes to procedures or responsibilities (including project sustainability goals and requirements) resulting from the pre-construction conference.

PARTNERING

Depending on the project's size, type, and complexity, the team may benefit from a partnering approach to promote cooperation, minimize arguments, and quickly resolve disputes. Establishing these relationships builds trust and the team shares risk, allowing for a more efficient operation.

DOCUMENTATION OF EXISTING CONDITIONS

Given the potentially litigious nature of construction projects, the CM can minimize the potential damage of claims with a thorough review of existing conditions of property impacted by construction. The CM conducts a walkthrough of the project site and documents the condition of existing structures and other areas of note. Photographs or videos can record this inspection with a date stamp to preserve a baseline of existing conditions before construction.

ASSIGNMENT OF OWNER FURNISHED ITEMS

To obtain time or cost savings or ensure product control, the owner may contract separately for certain long lead or specialty items.

During construction, the CM helps the owner establish the transfer procedures for owner-provided materials and equipment. This requires identifying specific personnel (either contractor or owner) who are responsible for supplier administration and determining responsibility for delivery coordination, shipping charges, insurance, receipt, unloading, storage, and installation. The CM should also review the material delivery schedules and their relation to the overall project schedule to ensure that owner-furnished equipment does not delay the project.

PERMITS, INSURANCE, LABOR AFFIDAVITS, AND BONDS

The CM should monitor the contractor's progress in securing proof of insurance, permits, bonds, and labor affidavits. The CM must closely track administrative submittals to ensure that the contractor meets scheduled submittal dates and should ensure that the contractor does not begin work until securing the required permits, insurance, etc.

The CM should receive copies of all documents that the contractor secures and review each for compliance with the specifications. This includes copies of all bonds the contractor secures to include payment and performance bonds. The CM should also receive copies of insurance certificates the contractor secures, including builder's risk, general liability, workman's compensation, and railroad or other owner-specific required policies. This may also include professional liability insurance if the project is under a design-build delivery arrangement.

Insurance policies should name the owner and CM as additional insured. The dollar limits should be commensurate with the scope of work performed. The CM should verify that subcontractors also have the specified insurance coverage.

COMMUNICATION PROCEDURES

The CM should prepare communication procedures to ensure the prompt and efficient exchange of information. Initially, the CM should create and distribute a project directory to include all key project personnel with their addresses, telephone numbers, fax numbers, email addresses, and cell numbers in case of an emergency. The CM should also prepare a submittal flow chart and matrices which indicate who has responsibility and authority for different aspects of the project, including the project's sustainability requirements.

The CM should also coordinate the:

- » RFI procedure.
- » Deficiency reporting procedure.
- » Payment application procedures.
- » Request/authorization procedures for changed or additional work.

MEETINGS

The CM should arrange and conduct periodic meetings to review the progress of the work in the field, along with any project sustainability requirements. These usually occur monthly, but different project phases may require more frequent meetings. Meetings should include reviews of the CPM schedules, outstanding or potential problems, possible solutions, current versus budgeted line items, technical issues, project sustainability requirements, and safety concerns. The meetings should also verify timely responses to submittals, RFIs, and redesign requests.

Each progress meeting should include sustainability goal progress and, from the beginning, some meetings should focus specifically on sustainability goals. The frequency of these meetings will increase as the project nears completion. At these meetings, the team should review scorecards, documentation status, and all potential open credits that the team may obtain.

The CM creates a project meeting plan as well as prepares and distributes meeting notices and agendas to all parties before the meetings. The CM also prepares and distributes minutes accordingly. Minutes have an action list detailing items requiring follow-up, the parties responsible, and the expected schedule for action. The CM also maintains a list of open issues that the project team works to resolve.

DOCUMENTATION PROCEDURES

Before the actual start of construction, the CM should establish project documentation requirements. These should include any sustainability documentation requirements. Complete documentation of construction progress and all relevant surrounding events is necessary because any project can become the subject of lengthy claims and litigation. Written documentation can help reconstruct the actual events that occurred, so its existence adds tremendous credibility to any testimony, opinion, or evaluation that an individual or firm may provide.

The actual work activity performance record (how long, using what forces, and under what conditions) is valuable when evaluating and negotiating contractor requests for additional time and compensation. A written record that documents the use of proper materials and methods is also valuable if there are questions later about construction quality.

The CM should establish a project documentation system capable of recording, storing, and retrieving information pertaining to all technical, financial, and administrative project aspects. While all projects are unique and have different recordkeeping requirements, certain types of information are typical of all types of construction projects.

COMPUTERIZED INFORMATION MANAGEMENT

The CM's goal is to provide timely information to the project team about the project's overall status and forecasts that compare the expected outcome to the baseline plan. Smaller projects with a CM staff of one or two might not need a high-end computerized MIS, but every project will benefit from some form of a computerized system to track the construction progress and to store data for future use.

There are many off-the-shelf software packages that exist specifically for this purpose. In addition, many CM firms have their own software systems that are particular to the type of construction they manage. Proper training is necessary for any computerized MIS because software effectiveness depends on the capabilities of the person inputting the data. (See **Chapter 9: Technology Management**.)

QUALITY CONTROL

Starting in the design phase, the CM should continuously monitor quality control. This includes review, certification, inspection, and testing of project components to determine if they conform to the plans, specifications, applicable standards, and project requirements.

Components include:

» Persons	» Documents
» Systems	» Techniques
» Materials	» Workmanship

QUALITY ASSURANCE

For QA, the CM applies planned and systemic methods to verify that QC procedures are being effectively implemented. The CM may also need to confirm that the project engaged a CA when required.

QA/QC METHODS

There are various project QA/QC methods. Some agencies/owners have preferred methods, but no one plan is best. The type of project and delivery system will often determine the most appropriate method. The goal is to verify that the work is in accordance with the construction contract documents, shop drawings, and installation procedures, as well as provides the owner with the specified level of quality. The most widely used methods include:

» The CM provides QA and the contractor provides QC.

» The CM and owner both evaluate the contractor's QC process to ensure it is applied properly and measures what is truly important for the project's quality.

QUALITY CONTROL MANUAL

Regardless of the QA/QC method, establishing a formal plan (usually as part of the CMP) improves the process. The CM should either review the contractor's plan or develop one if necessary. The plan should emphasize inspection, test control, scheduling, testing and operating status, certification of records, corrective action, and audits. The preparation and review must be done in accordance with the specifications. Requiring more stringent testing may result in changes or delays and significant added expense.

For more, see *CMAA Quality Management Guidelines*.

FIELD REPORTS

The CM should ensure that the project has an adequate daily reporting system. **The daily report is the most important element in the documentation of an ongoing construction project.** All personnel with supervisory control of construction (such as project managers, trade or area superintendents, project engineers, and inspectors) prepare daily reports.

The supervisor should promptly review daily reports. Any items requiring attention should be attended to promptly and so noted on the original inspection report. At the time of review, the supervisor notes and initials modifications to the original report. Any required weekly or monthly reporting should appropriately summarize the information in the daily reports.

SAFETY

The contractor and its subcontractors have ultimate responsibility for safety, but in the current legal environment, the CM and owner must stay involved. Many owners request that CMs take a larger role in safety management, but many insurers advise CMs to take a smaller role. The CM should monitor the implementation of the contractor's safety program to minimize accidents and the owner's exposure if they occur.

The CM reviews the contractor's safety plan but might not be responsible for implementation or compliance, depending on its contractual status (agency or at-risk). It is essential that the CM's CMP outlines a system that periodically evaluates and prepares a formal report on the contractor's compliance with its safety plan.

Components of the safety program should include the following:

» Safety meetings
» Agency certification
» Personal protective equipment
» A safety awards program
» Safety inspections

CHANGE MANAGEMENT

The basic construction contract clearly sets forth the rights and obligations of the parties thereto. The contractor has a duty to complete the project that the detailed technical plans and specifications prescribe and must do this in accordance with the contract's terms and provisions. The owner has a legally enforceable right to this performance. In return, the owner is bound to pay the contractor an agreed value (most are fixed-price contracts but may be other types, such as unit price or cost-plus-percentage contracts) for successful project completion. The contractor has a corresponding legally enforceable right to such payment.

Much of the CM's participation in construction contract administration involves contract changes and modifications. During construction, change requests may come from the owner, the contractor, the designer, third parties, or the CM. The CM should respond to changes in the work in a timely manner. The CM should analyze each change request, prepare the necessary information for justification, and then submit an assessment to the owner or designer with a recommended action.

Certain procedures can reduce problems if the contract documents include them or if all parties agree to them early on. These include requiring the contractor to promptly notify the CM in writing of any changed conditions, omissions, or discrepancies that may result in extra work. This also includes the owner or designer promptly notifying the CM of any desired design modifications.

The CMP should clearly identify members of the CM's staff that are able to authorize changes to the scope of work, the schedule, and the method of performing the work. Beginning any extra work should require written direction.

COST CONTROL

The CM should establish and maintain a computerized cost control system. The system should include a cost database and a cost analysis method to track change requests and claims estimates, actual contractor bid prices, and contractor progress payments. The system should also be compatible with the owner's systems and accurately track the overall budget, including costs to complete changes, force account work, and cash flow projections.

For more information, see *CMAA Cost Management Guidelines*.

SCHEDULE MONITORING

The CM performs scheduling duties to effectively monitor the project's progress and coordinate the project team. These duties include reviewing the contractor's schedule, the schedule of consultants, and the designer's time-sensitive services, as well as analyzing time extension requests, tracking force account work, and reporting monthly progress.

> **Initial Review** - The CM reviews the contractor's baseline schedule to confirm it meets the specifications and the master schedule. Schedule conflicts are identified and resolved. Conflicts with the owner and third parties should be mutually resolved to develop a schedule acceptable to all parties. The master schedule should incorporate the approved baseline schedule.

> **Monthly Updates** – The contractor's approved baseline schedule should receive updates at least monthly. To help eliminate misunderstanding and incorrect information, the CM and contractor must establish a process to jointly review the updated information before updating the schedule. During the review, the CM should check the specifications to determine if the schedule update complies with revision requirements and verify that the written narrative describes the progress accurately.

Preparing Monthly Updates

- ✓ Input the progress data and re-run the schedule
- ✓ Check the current project milestones and completion
- ✓ Prepare monthly report and submit for approval
- ✓ Owner reviews for accuracy and approval
- ✓ If behind schedule, identify delays and entitlement for time extensions and evaluate alternatives for recovery

PROGRESS PAYMENTS

Unless one exists under the owner's current operations, the CM should establish a system to control contractor payments that is consistent with the owner's objectives and requirements. Progress payments are based on the actual amount of work performed through the period of the payment request. The contract specifications typically establish the method of payment.

Common methods include:

» Unit prices

» Schedule of values

» Cost-loaded CPM schedule

» Cost reimbursable (cost plus)

Each method has its advantages, disadvantages, and peculiarities, but there are general procedures common to all arrangements.

The contractor must submit its proposed payment breakdown to the CM for approval before receiving the NTP. In the case of a unit price contract, this is part of the bid package. The submission should divide the project into reasonable work packages for easy identification and verification. It should also include estimated quantities of the completed work, where appropriate.

The CM then reviews the contractor's proposed payment breakdown and should verify that each item's proposed value is reasonable. Unbalanced payment schedules can create serious problems, so the CM should resolve any questions with the contractor before the first payment.

The owner should also review and approve the payment schedule before the first payment.

STATUS REPORTS

The CM should establish a reporting system to inform the owner of project events and progress. The project's PPM usually establishes the type, format, and frequency of reports. Reports should include:

» Schedule

» Cost

» Cash flow projection

» Executive summary

» Sustainability goals

CLAIMS MITIGATION/EVALUATION

Proactively implementing all the previously discussed procedures will help avoid or mitigate most issues. On large projects, establishing a Disputes Review Board can also help resolve disputes at the project level. Unfortunately, claims can occur on even well-run construction projects. The CM should receive and evaluate all notices of claims by the contractor and recommend action to the owner in a timely manner. A claim evaluation is usually divided into two distinct parts: an entitlement evaluation and a damages assessment.

ENTITLEMENT EVALUATION

The contractor submits its claim notification to the CM. This notification may or may not include the contractor's proposed settlement value. If the contractor provides a verbal notice of claim, the project records should document it and the CM should advise the contractor to provide written notice immediately. Upon receipt of written notification from the contractor, the CM responds in writing, acknowledging receipt and requesting any appropriate additional information required for evaluation. The owner should receive copies of this correspondence.

DAMAGES ASSESSMENT

If determined that the contractor's claim has merit, the determination of damages can start. All pertinent records should be retrieved, copied, numbered, and retained in a separate file dedicated to the claim. With these records, the CM assesses the full impact to the contractor that is attributable to its claim. The CM should analyze both the claim's direct and indirect costs to determine the total compensation due to the contractor. During the damages analysis, it may be in the best interest of all parties to meet with the contractor to obtain information and explore potential forms of settlement.

AS-BUILT DRAWINGS

The CM establishes procedures to assemble and handle record drawings as well as reviews these drawings before approving final payment. It is important to capture and continuously post information that reflects the project's actual as-built condition.

The construction contract typically requires the contractor to maintain a set of hard copy as-built drawings (by marking all changes from the original drawings as bid), which the CM periodically reviews for completeness. The condition of the as-built drawings is often part of the pay application process. Many facility designs use a BIM environment, so the owner will want the BIM model to reflect the as-built condition. The CM must understand the contract's requirements for who should update the BIM model and when those updates must occur.

PUNCHLISTS

The CM normally provides for inspection of the project work, noting both the status and quality of work in place. A punchlist notes items that require corrective action. The contractors are required to make corrections. This process is continuous. All punchlist items must be remedied before a project closes out and the owner accepts it.

If a punchlist item will delay future construction or work will cover it over, immediate remedial action should occur. The CM manages corrective action. The owner or the designer will also inspect and may add items to the punchlist when the contractor declares substantial completion.

COMMISSIONING (CX) AND FUNCTIONAL PERFORMANCE TESTING

The commissioning agent (CA) leads the commissioning team that performs final testing on all the project's operational equipment. The CA documents these tests and logs any deficiencies. Each project's original contract specifications, size, and complexity will determine the level of commissioning. Some projects may also not have an independent CA. The project must clear all deficiencies before the commissioning process is complete.

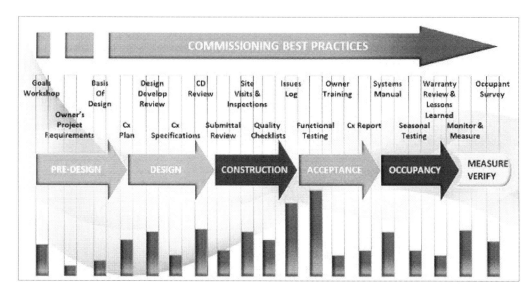

Figure 2: Chart provided courtesy of Jim Ogden & 3QC ©

6.6 Post-Construction Phase

This phase provides the bridge between construction and a facility's operation. It is important to perform this transition smoothly. Achieving a successful CMP during the design and construction phases limits problems in the post-construction phase and creates a mechanism for the project's timely closeout. During this phase, the CM helps archive project documentation, completes administrative contract closeouts, initiates occupancy of the completed facility, and provides for warranty enforcement processes.

CHECKLIST AND SCHEDULE

The post-construction checklist helps manage the post-construction process. The CM should use the project's sustainability plan and governing management guidance (the QMP, PMP, etc.) to develop a post-construction checklist.

The post-construction checklist must also identify sustainable design and construction processes if the project seeks to achieve sustainability goals or comply with sustainability requirements. It must also include documentation requirements, such as sustainable design or construction rating systems' requirements, sustainable guidelines, or high-performance code requirements.

OPERATION AND MAINTENANCE (O&M) MANUALS

The CM uses the document control system's submittal section to track and verify that the owner receives the maintenance manuals and operations procedures that the contractor develops. The CM should also coordinate training for the owner's staff in how to operate contractor-installed equipment. The CM defines the training procedures and schedules, monitors, and documents the training sessions.

OPERATIONS PERSONNEL TRAINING

Training for facilities operators, maintenance personnel, and owners may be necessary for equipment, assets, and models or computer-based management systems that lend to a project's "sustainability" characteristics. The contract documents, any commissioning plans, and the post-occupancy checklist should specify appropriate training. Training must finish before closeout. The introduction of every training program should reiterate the project's overall sustainable goals and clearly articulate how the equipment or asset relates to these objectives.

SPARE PARTS AND WARRANTIES

The CM coordinates the submittal of the specified spare parts (also called attic stock) and the contractor's warranties to the owner. The document control system's submittal section helps monitor progress. The owner's staff should help develop a system for transferring, cataloging, and storing spare parts. The owner should also receive all warranties and guarantee information in a logical format. A comprehensive checklist should include all constructed items having a warranty or spare part requirement.

FINAL PERMITS

The CM oversees the acquisition of all required operating permits and compliance with regulatory requirements. The CM coordinates any required agency inspections and securing occupancy permits. The document control system's submittal section should track the status of all permits.

SUSTAINABLE PROJECT DOCUMENTATION

Project teams pursuing Leadership in Energy and Environmental Design (LEED) certification from the U.S. Green Building Council, Green Globes certification from the Green Building Institute, or compliance with any other sustainable design or construction rating system must register their project in accordance with applicable requirements, typically before construction begins.

The CM must ensure that contractors provide documentation to meet all contractual obligations and certification requirements. The CM must begin to meet this responsibility before the post-construction phase and must remain diligent throughout the process to guarantee the contractors provide the documentation.

ACCEPTANCE, PERFORMANCE TESTING, AND COMMISSIONING

The CM must often monitor the performance testing and acceptance of specified systems to verify that they satisfy the contract requirements. The general contractor must file all appropriate test reports and provide the CM access to watch these tests.

Building systems commissioning ensures that systems operate according to design intent and that they provide proper indoor air quality, comfort, and energy efficiency. The commissioning process theoretically yields a properly functioning facility, professionally-trained operations staff, and documentation that describes the system's design intent and commissioning procedures.

BENEFICIAL OCCUPANCY

Beneficial occupancy is the construction stage before final completion when the owner can occupy a facility for its intended purpose. The date of beneficial occupancy normally marks the beginning of the specified period on the guarantees. After beneficial occupancy, the owner must assume responsibility for the facility's maintenance and operation.

The CM often coordinates the owner's move-in to the completed project and the startup of project systems. The CM should help the owner develop an occupancy plan for the completed project that best suits its schedule and operational needs. To execute the process smoothly, the CM and owner must carefully plan and communicate phased occupancy requirements.

CLAIMS RESOLUTION

The CM should continue to help the owner resolve any outstanding claims brought by the designer or the contractor. Disputes and their resolutions are often a difficult, time-consuming, and disruptive part of a project that may continue long after construction finishes.

CONTRACTOR CLOSEOUT AND FINAL PAYMENT

The CM, the owner, and the designer conduct a final joint assessment of the project to verify that all work is complete. This involves implementing the PPM and the CMP's project closeout procedures. The CMP will establish the parameters to determine if the project is ready for the final inspection and how to perform the final inspection. The CMP will also establish the acceptance criteria that permit final payment.

CLOSEOUT REPORT

The owner should require the CM to prepare a project closeout report with specific contents. The CM prepares this final project report with all pertinent project data, including a summary of schedule and cost information. The report's written narrative provides a brief project history. Attachments should include all reports issued during the project in final form. The report should also note the date of substantial and final completion as well as the commencement date for all warranties.

CONTRACTOR WARRANTY RESPONSIBILITIES

The CM may continue to coordinate contractor response to warranty items as identified by the owner's O&M staff, but this is not always cost-effective. At a minimum, the CM should provide the owner with a list of key contacts for warranty or maintenance work.

POST-OCCUPANCY REVIEW FOR ENERGY PERFORMANCE CONTRACTS

For projects that employ energy performance contracts, the post-occupancy performance review involves testing a facility's performance with systems in full operation during a specified period after construction ends. Energy performance contracts typically specify the duration, performance criteria, performance testing protocols, and associated incentives or penalties.

PROJECT CLOSEOUT

Once the construction phase is complete, several closeout procedures are necessary to finish the project. While most project closeout tasks take place during the post-construction phase (after the contractor declares substantial completion), CMs should plan for closeout throughout the project, starting with the closeout requirements in the initial contract specifications. The contract must include any unique needs at the project's beginning to avoid potential issues. Careful planning in the pre-design phase helps closeout go smoothly, with fewer frustrations and delays.

PRE-CLOSEOUT MEETING

The CM chairs the pre-closeout meeting to kick off the project's final phase. This meeting should occur well before the end of the project. The attendees should include the contractor and the owner who will operate the completed project.

SUBSTANTIAL COMPLETION

The contractor will notify the CM after reaching substantial completion. The CM should confirm that the necessary tasks are adequately complete. After confirming substantial completion, the project can begin final closeout procedures.

The building official's final code inspection sometimes accompanies or is a requirement for substantial completion. This also begins the closeout process for the remaining open permits.

CLOSEOUT PROCEDURES

These closeout procedures ensure that completed construction tasks conform to the contract documents. This involves more than handing off the project to the owner. It includes checking necessary punchlists, reviewing and submitting completed paperwork, and double-checking all specified obligations.

FINAL MILESTONE COMPLETION

When the project reaches this milestone, the contractor completed construction as required in the contract documents. This is often when the owner provides final payment to the contractor. The closeout punchlist and all the closeout procedures are successfully complete. All required tasks are complete. The CM finished reviewing all documentation given to the owner. The certificate of occupancy has been issued and all inspections are complete. The facility is ready for occupancy.

For more, see *CMAA Project Closeout Guidelines.*

Notes

Notes

CHAPTER 7

Safety Management

7.1   Responsibility for Jobsite Safety

The CM reviews the contractor's safety plan but might not be responsible for implementation or compliance, depending on its contractual status (agency or at-risk). A project must develop a system that periodically evaluates the contractor's compliance with its safety plan and periodically prepares a formal report on such. The CM's CMP should outline these procedures.

The CM should report identified safety violations and monitor their correction. The report should include the name of the contractor; the time, date, and location of the hazard; the reason why the observer believes a hazard exists; and a reference to the applicable Occupational Safety and Health Administration (OSHA) regulation or other regulation.

The contractor's safety program includes methods to prevent accidents, reduce hazards, implement site safety management, conduct safety training, and enforce regulatory compliance. A project's senior safety review team includes the safety director of the affected agency (railroad, department of transportation, etc.), the CM, the contractor's safety supervisor, and the insurance carrier's safety representative.

7.2   Introduction

This section focuses on providing the required safety management services to the owner. Generally, the CM's obligation to provide safety services varies from project to project. The contract between the owner and CM must clearly specify them. The CM reviews the contractor's proposed agreement with the owner to ensure that no contract language specifies CM safety obligations or responsibilities besides those clearly defined in the CM agreement.

This section's approach to safety management is proactive. The CM and owner must note that the approach described here is much more aggressive than other standard forms of agreement available from various providers. This proactive approach can be appropriate for providing comprehensive safety services to owners who are willing to provide the CM with the appropriate compensation, insurance coverage, and contract indemnification clauses.

Terminology

Accident

Incident

Gambling

Near miss

Hazard

Risk

Risk assessment

Job hazard analysis (JHA)

Job safety analysis (JSA)

Before providing any safety management services, the CM thoroughly reviews all legal implications of doing so and understands the risks associated with this service. On some projects, the CM should consider indemnification clauses and insurance coverage for safety issues even if not providing the services described in this section. At a minimum, CMs must follow the safety policy and practices of their own organization.

NOTE: The owner and the CM should also note other available safety management options. Depending on the owner's resources, these options include:

1. If an owner has a well-established safety program or organization, the owner can provide a safety coordinator to perform the noted project safety functions and interface accordingly with the CM.

2. If neither the owner nor CM has an established safety program or organization with the resources to serve as a safety coordinator, a safety consultant may provide the functions of the safety coordinator and interface appropriately with the owner and CM.

The construction management company is ultimately responsible for the safety of its employees. The company must have a safety program in place for its employees in accordance with the local laws and regulations. This program should include education and training for the CM staff commensurate with company policy and the hazards expected during the construction. The program should also consider specific contract terms and delivery method details.

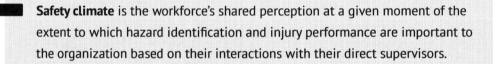

Safety climate is the workforce's shared perception at a given moment of the extent to which hazard identification and injury performance are important to the organization based on their interactions with their direct supervisors.

7.3   Pre-Design Phase

The CM must discuss and thoroughly understand the owner's commitment level to an overall safety program for jobsite construction work. The owner has the overall responsibility for action if the nature of a hazard or safety responsibilities between the CM and contractor present an issue.

If the owner lacks a strong commitment to safety, the CM **may not** want to take a contractual safety role on the project. The CM and owner should discuss the advantages and disadvantages of doing so, as well as the current governmental requirements, expectations, and the project's established goals.

If the CM will implement and organize a safety program, the CM's contract with the owner must clearly define the scope of such services and include compensation to cover the CM's cost for appropriate liability protection. **The prudent CM negotiates a separate fee for providing safety management services that should include the added cost to acquire additional insurance coverage.** The following information assumes that the owner requested and contracted with the CM to provide an overall jobsite safety program.

INITIAL SCOPE OF SERVICES FOR CM PROVIDING AN OVERALL JOBSITE SAFETY PROGRAM

The CM reviews the owner's standard contract documents to determine if the language achieves the owner's safety goals and meets the CM's contractual safety requirements. The CM's safety services scope can vary by contract from periodic observation and monitoring to more detailed monitoring, documenting, and reporting the contractor's safety progress.

The project team should prioritize safety issues first and resolve them in a timely manner. The CM must clearly explain to the owner that anyone on the CM staff who witnesses a safety hazard will bring the issue to the contractor for corrective action. If the CM encounters an imminent danger situation, the contract must empower the CM to suspend work on that activity immediately on behalf of the owner, who is ultimately responsible for the suspension.

PROJECT ORGANIZATION

The CM's safety coordinator should be an early member of the project team. The safety coordinator develops safety input for items such as the CMP, PPM, pre-construction drawings, constructability reviews, and the MIS.

STAFFING CONSIDERATIONS

To coordinate and monitor contractor safety efforts effectively, the CM creates a separate safety staff within the construction management team. The safety staff are safety professionals with project-specific experience and knowledge of the following:

» Federal, state, county, and local safety regulations

» Building Officials and Code Administrators (BOCA) and National Fire Protection Association (NFPA) codes

» American National Standards Institute (ANSI) standards

» Occupational Safety and Health Administration (OSHA) regulations

» Environmental Protection Agency (EPA), Distributed Energy Resource (DER), and other environmental regulations

» Hazard communications requirements

» Construction operations, specifications, and drawings

» Labor relations

Some projects with special jobsite conditions (e.g., asbestos abatement or remediation, or hazardous waste removal) may require a Certified Safety Professional (CSP), Construction Health and Safety Technician (CHST), and Certified Industrial Hygienist (CIH). The owner must understand why the project staff needs experienced safety professionals. The staff's size must adequately and efficiently cover the project as well as fulfill the agreed contract scope.

7.4 Design Phase

The CM safety coordinator meets with the design team to understand the project's scope. At this time, the safety coordinator can review drawings and discuss specific project elements to determine potential safety hazards after the project begins. "Design for construction safety" is an industry phrase that means teams should consider safety during the project's design. For example, window elevations, parapet wall heights, and construction sequencing can all help to prevent construction accidents.

The CM safety coordinator may then provide input to the construction contract documents concerning specific safety devices, equipment, and training that may be necessary to mitigate potential hazards. For example, certain roof designs may require special fall arresting devices and safety nets. Trenches and excavations also have specific safety equipment requirements. Instead of relying on the successful bidder's discretion, all participants benefit more if the contract documents require specialized equipment.

The contract should clearly state that the contractor has the primary responsibility to perform its own review of the drawings to determine potential hazards. Any contract guidelines shall be considered a minimum requirement. The contractors must then devise systems or obtain necessary protective equipment at no additional cost to the owner. In addition, the contract may require the contractor to provide protective equipment to the owner's inspection team.

The owner's legal counsel should review and incorporate indemnification clauses and insurance requirements into the contractor's contract documents. The intent is to protect the owner and CM from liability for safety-related claims.

CONTRACT SAFETY REQUIREMENTS AND DRAFTING GUIDELINES

The CM safety coordinator determines the safety items to include in the construction contract documents based on the owner's safety programs, the review conducted during the design phase, and the CM's role during construction. The contract documents should ensure that the prime contractors and subcontractors are responsible for safety.

Submittals

Based on the contract requirements and the appropriate project characteristics, prime contractors may need to submit the following information to the CM for review:

- » Written safety program
- » Résumé of safety representative and applicable certifications
- » Hazard communication program
- » Specialized programs for specific job hazards
- » Environmental waste disposal plan
- » Drug and alcohol program (where required)
- » Safety training programs

» Union safety regulations (where applicable)

» Site-specific safety plan

» Task-specific safety and health plans for high-risk activities

Responsibilities and Requirements

The contract documents should clearly state that the contractor is solely responsible for the safety and welfare of its employees and for the protection of property and the public. The contract documents should clearly establish the contractor's responsibilities and requirements to:

» Comply with all federal, state, local, and county safety regulations applicable to the project scope and the worksite.

» Provide a safety representative who shall be a full-time employee of the contractor and whose responsibility shall be to supervise compliance with applicable safety requirements on the worksite and to develop and implement safety training classes for all job personnel. The safety representative shall have stop work authority.

» With a safety representative, ensure that all subcontractors of any tier fully comply with the prime contractor's jobsite safety program.

» Require subcontractors to comply with jurisdictional requirements that may require full-time safety representatives.

» Recognize the owner's authority to remove the contractor's safety representative if the owner judges that the representative is improperly or inadequately performing their duties, but that authority should not affect the contractor's responsibility to perform the work safely, nor shall it impose any obligation upon the owner, the owner's CM, or any other party besides the contractor to ensure the contractor performs work safely.

WRITTEN SAFETY PROGRAM

The jobsite safety program is a critical part of the contractor's safety effort. The contractor's safety program should include everything the contractor needs to administer the program and meet the contract's requirements.

At a minimum, the contractor's written safety program should address:

» **Compliance with laws, rules, and regulations (including any updates), to include:**

  - Federal, state, and local laws.

  - Owner, CM, insurance carriers.

  - 100% safety orientation of all jobsite personnel and visitors (verifiable tracking system, can be through visual sticker identification on hard hats).

» **Duties and responsibilities of contractor's management personnel for safety, including the:**
- PM.
- General superintendent.
- Supervisor (Foreman).
- Safety manager/representative.
- Safety committee or team(s).

» **Policies for infractions of safety rules, including:**
- Life-threatening (imminent danger) situations corrected immediately.
- Serious hazards.
- Infractions reported to the contractor's designated safety representative.
- Timely correction.
- Prime contractors to enforce safety requirements on their subcontractors.
- The contractor to remove non-complying employees from the project on their own or at the request of the owner/CM.

» **Housekeeping policies, such as:**
- Continuous cleaning required.
- Final clean-up required.
- The owner will perform if required and charge contractors.
- A designated staging plan.

» **Means of implementing the program, including:**
- The CM representative attends weekly toolbox meetings with the agenda recorded.
- Incorporate safety in weekly project meetings; ask questions to help the contractor plan safety into the work.
- Implement a safety committee or safety walkaround inspections with the contractor.
- Distribute emergency procedures and phone numbers.
- Post a project bulletin board with required policies.
- Employees on each shift should have first aid/CPR training and maintain a current first aid/CPR card issued by an agency such as the American Red Cross.
- Completion of a job hazard analysis for each critical non-routine or high hazard construction activity and communication of this analysis to workers through pre-installation meetings for each recent activity.
- Have an accessible safety program manual.

Why Safety?
✓ Invest in your most valuable asset: people
✓ Identify and manage your risks
✓ Save money
− Direct costs
− Indirect costs
✓ Industry recognition
✓ Experience modification rate (EMR)

- Promote effective communication with a means of elevating safety issues to upper management for resolution.
- Establish tracking and recordkeeping procedures.
- Conduct accident investigation.

» **Procedures to investigate, document, and report all accidents and near-misses, such as:**
- Steps to prevent a recurrence.
- Completion of all reporting paperwork.
- Proper notification and distribution.

The contract documents should state the contractor's compliance with safety requirements and CM's or owner's review of the contractor's safety program shall not relieve or decrease the contractor's liability for safety.

The contract documents should only make the contractor responsible for safety, not the owner, CM, or any other party. The contractor should indemnify, defend, and hold harmless the owner, CM, or other authorized owner's representatives, from and against all actions, damages, fines, suits, and losses resulting from the contractor's failure to meet all safety requirements and provide a safe worksite.

7.5 Procurement Phase

PRE-BID CONFERENCE

The pre-bid conference can provide the CM's safety representative or owner safety representative an opportunity to address potential bidders. The representative highlights the contract's safety requirements at this time.

SAFETY AS A PREQUALIFICATION CRITERION

The CM helps the owner consider contractors' safety records as criteria for prequalification to bid on projects for that owner. These records should include the contractor's:

» Lost time frequency average.

» Lost time severity average.

» OSHA 200 and 300 form information.

» OSHA Recordable Incident Rates (RIR).

» Experience modification rate (interstate or state EMR, determined by the state Worker's Compensation Board).

This information can help to screen bidders with poor safety programs that may cause the owner increased worker's compensation costs. This is particularly important when the owner provides an Owner Controlled Insurance Program (OCIP). The contractor must also provide an up-to-date list of all their OSHA/state citations within the past three years that includes the disposition of each citation. Citation information is available on the OSHA website (www.osha.gov) under "Establishment Search."

EMR / Incident Rate Calculation

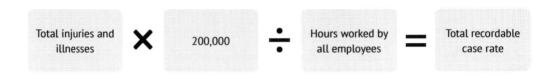

| Total injuries and illnesses | **✕** | 200,000 | **÷** | Hours worked by all employees | **=** | Total recordable case rate |

EMERGENCY RESPONSE COORDINATION

The CM safety representative contacts local authorities before bid to determine the availability of ambulance service, emergency response, police, and fire units.

The contractor's safety manager establishes emergency response procedures, means, and methods after the owner awards the construction contract.

7.6   Construction Phase

SAFETY SUBMITTALS

The CM reviews the contractor's safety-related submittals to determine if the contract specification requirements are met. The CM's review is not intended to be all-encompassing nor to anticipate each jobsite condition the contractor may encounter.

The contract provisions should say that no work can begin until the safety program's submission. The contractor's submitted program is the contractor's and subcontractors' main safety compliance element. The contractor's plan should include documentation of competent persons assigned to the project.

For some projects/programs, it may be appropriate to allow a two-stage safety program submittal. One stage covers the first 90 days for mobilization and the second covers the contract's remainder.

CMs should develop their own safety program for construction management employees on the jobsite. The jobsite could expose construction management employees to many of the same hazards as contractor personnel. Therefore, it is good practice to provide and document training for the CM's personnel. At a minimum, the CM should comply with the prime contractor's jobsite safety program.

COMPLIANCE AGENCIES

Both the owner and CM should develop lines of communication with agencies that enforce regulations that apply to the project's construction. The CM can encourage contractors that work on the project to meet with these agencies. Before construction starts, a best practice is to review the project scope and contractual relationships among the owner, CM, and prime contractors.

PRE-CONSTRUCTION CONFERENCE

The CM's safety representative addresses all prime contractors at the pre-construction conference. At this time, the conference should review the following information with the contractors:

» Submittal requirements

» Emergency response programs and procedures

» Safety meeting times and schedules

» Training requirements

» Site safety surveys

» Accident investigations

» Reporting procedures

The meeting should remind the contractor to transmit all safety-related materials to all subcontractors of any tier. Language in the contractor's contract should require the contractor to provide adequate documentation for safety. This language should also extend to all subcontractors. The contractor should conduct additional meetings with subcontractors to review the information from the initial pre-construction meeting.

CONTRACTOR SAFETY ENFORCEMENT AND COMPLIANCE

Each contractor's safety representative should help the contractor's management personnel implement the contractor's jobsite safety program. Every day, the safety representative and contractor's management personnel inspect their construction activity for compliance with their established work plans, processes, and procedures, as well as document their findings.

The CM monitors the contractor's daily construction activities and notifies the contractor in writing (with copies to the owner) of any deficiencies, hazards, or situations observed. Hazards must be addressed immediately, orally, and with the CM's authority to stop work if workers or other personnel are potentially in danger. The CM follows up with the contractor to determine if corrective measures were taken. The CM's actions in this regard are not intended to relieve the contractors of their responsibilities for jobsite safety.

The CM immediately notifies the owner if the contractor fails to correct an unsafe condition. The owner then notifies the contractor through the CM that the unsafe condition must be corrected or the work in question stops until the condition is corrected to the owner's satisfaction. The contractor does not receive time extensions or additional compensation because of any stop work order issued under these circumstances. While an unsafe condition continues, someone may be at risk.

SAFETY COORDINATION MEETINGS

Before starting any critical, high hazard, or non-routine (as defined by the contract or contractor's submitted safety plan) construction activities, the contractor must perform a job hazard analysis (JHA). The JHA outlines the contractor's plans and procedures to perform the work in a safe manner. The CM and contractor(s) discuss the JHA at a safety coordinator meeting. At this time, the contractor thoroughly reviews the work in question and ensures that all concerned parties receive safety guidelines. The contractor must use the JHA to conduct training and hold meetings with the contractor's employees before performing the work.

SAFETY COMMITTEE

The CM serves on the jobsite safety committee. The committee may also include the owner's safety manager and contractor's safety and management representatives. The committee meets at least once a month to review safety issues and contractor jobsite progress. The agendas for the meetings should include:

» The results and recommendations of weekly committee walkaround inspections, or other project safety inspections.

» A review of the contractor's safety/training activities.

» A review and update of jobsite emergency procedures and access routes.

» Coordination of hazard communication information for compliance with the federal hazard communication standard.

» A review of accidents and near-misses on-site as well as steps implemented to prevent a recurrence.

» A look at anticipated construction activity to determine if safety coordination between contractors should take place.

» A review of contractor accident rates in conjunction with national standards.

SAFETY AUDITS

If specified in the CM contract, the CM conducts periodic safety audits to monitor contractor progress and compliance with the following:

» Orientation training

» Hazard communication training

» Accident investigations

» Jobsite inspection

» Emergency procedures

» Disciplinary action

» Safety meetings

» Overall administration of their safety program

The contractor should participate in the CM audit and be allowed to take immediate corrective action if appropriate. The owner also receives an audit report for review and appropriate action. The audit's purpose is to document observed areas where the contractor or subcontractors are in or out of compliance with the contractor's jobsite or project safety program.

The audit is not an all-inclusive listing of safety conditions on the project. In addition, the safety audit's suggestions are intended only to notify the contractor of observed instances when it is not in compliance with its own safety program. The safety audit reminds the contractor of the obligation to comply with the safety program, including the regulations, laws, and ordinances referenced in the program.

MONTHLY REPORTS

The CM provides monthly reports to the owner containing the program's status as well as accident frequency and severity.

CM SAFETY TRAINING

The CM should initially train and periodically refresh training for construction management employees on how to identify and avoid hazards on the construction site, per their jobsite safety program. CMs have responsibility for their own employees' safety on contractor jobsites.

Notes

Notes

CHAPTER 8

Sustainability

8.1 Introduction

This section discusses the CM's role in the established and growing subject of sustainability. It outlines sustainability's key goals, philosophies, and elements in general terms. The general philosophy is that the overall project goals should incorporate sustainability principles and be key parts of the CMP. An industry consensus is that the key guiding principles for sustainable facilities should include the following five basic principles:

1. Employ integrated design principles.
2. Optimize energy performance.
3. Protect and conserve water.
4. Enhance indoor environmental quality.
5. Reduce the environmental impact of materials.

To incorporate sustainable principles, a project must include sustainable requirements beginning at an early stage of project planning and design that continue during construction. The CM must completely understand the requirements and follow through on their incorporation into the project.

There are a variety of sustainability rating systems that measure and document how well a facility or project meets sustainability requirements. Most rating systems apply to a range of building types, including both new and existing building projects. Green building rating systems are established tools that are becoming the standard to measure compliance with sustainability's key guiding principles. All owners, architects, CMs, and building managers should understand these systems. The industry now uses many sustainability rating systems, but the most common in the U.S. are LEED and Green Globes.

8.2 Pre-Design Phase

ESTABLISHING PROJECT SUSTAINABILITY GOALS

The CM helps the owner establish the project's sustainability goals and objectives. This important first step helps ensure the project stakeholders' roles and responsibilities align with the project's sustainability expectations. The CM includes the sustainability objectives, team responsibilities, and sustainability procedures in the project sustainability plan. The CM must have the necessary experience and qualifications to support the owner in this effort.

The project must establish its sustainability goals before the design starts. This includes deciding whether to register the project with a benchmark rating entity, such as the U.S. Green Building Council (USGBC).

CONTRACT DEVELOPMENT

The CM works with the owner's legal counsel to develop the design team's contract and should recommend appropriate language for the design phase's sustainability goals.

PROJECT MANAGEMENT PLAN (PMP)

The PMP should address the sustainability procedures for all project phases. The PMP should define the procedures necessary to ensure that each work phase achieves the sustainability criteria as well as project participants' roles and responsibilities.

PROJECT COMMISSIONING PLAN

If the construction management team employs the independent commissioning agent (CA), it is the CM's responsibility to develop the project commissioning plan. If other project participants employ the independent commissioning agent, the CM ensures that the project has a commissioning plan before design starts. In either case, the commissioning plan must satisfy the project's sustainability plan and the owner's sustainability requirements.

The CM reviews the plan to ensure it is applicable to the project and enforceable. The CM should review it for consistency with the master project schedule as well as the overall project goals and objectives. The commissioning plan should complement the project goals and objectives so that they focus on achieving the same project outcome.

PRE-DESIGN PROJECT CONFERENCE

The CM includes the project sustainability champion, sustainable design professionals, and commissioning agent in the pre-design conference. The meeting should review the project sustainability plan, including the project's sustainable goals and objectives. The conference should also clearly define and review the roles and responsibilities for project sustainability.

8.3   Design Phase

The owner and the CM should agree on the detailed scope and number of sustainability reviews required. The CM coordinates lifecycle analysis, alternative studies, and energy usage analysis. The CM regularly reviews published sustainability standards from the sustainability benchmark entity that are established project targets (such as LEED or Green Globes).

PROCUREMENT PHASE

Projects requiring certification with USGBC or Green Building Initiative (GBI) should include appropriate requirements in the bid documents. If the owner and designer choose NOT to formally register the project but intend for it to be equivalent to a LEED, Green Globes, or another certification, the bid documents must define the appropriate requirements.

It is the designer's responsibility to include the contractor's specific sustainable requirements. The contract drawings, specifications, and BIM documents should specifically identify these requirements. The bid documents should also include the minimum sustainability qualifications of bidders.

MEETINGS

The pre-proposal meeting should discuss sustainability. The meeting should specifically note whether the project will be a third-party certified project, the requirements for the contractor to ensure the project reaches the specified level of certification, and how to qualify bidder experience.

The CM helps the owner review the bids received. This includes a review of the bidders' specific, applicable sustainability experience as well as the qualification requirements in the bid documents.

8.4 Construction Phase

PRE-CONSTRUCTION CONFERENCE

A project should hold a separate pre-construction conference with the contractor if the project is registered with USGBC as LEED-certified or greater or with GBI for a specific number of Green Globes. The meeting should ensure the contractor clearly understands the project's sustainability documentation requirements.

If a project is not registered, the owner's team should still meet with the contractor to review responsible environmentally sustainable construction practices. The contractor should present the project's general approach and identify what sustainable construction practices the contractor will employ.

CONSTRUCTION PLANNING AND SCHEDULING

The contractor submits a schedule that should include a series of sustainability activities. If the project is registered with USGBC as LEED-certified or GBI Green Globes, monitoring and documentation may require more project activities or longer durations.

INSPECTION AND TESTING CONSISTENT WITH THE PROJECT COMMISSIONING PLAN (PCP)

The CM inspects the contractor's work daily to verify if the work satisfies environmental codes and regulations, the PCP, the contract documentation, and LEED, Green Globes, or other credit criteria. If the CM provides such services, these services should be defined in detail.

REPORTS AND RECORDKEEPING

The CM maintains thorough documentation of all the project's environmental measures. This includes but is not limited to the following:

- » Procurement of materials
- » Waste recycling
- » Waste reduction
- » Emissions mitigations
- » Noise and vibration mitigations
- » Dust reduction efforts

When the contract specifies that the CM must organize required documentation for a project that is built for certification to LEED, Green Globes, or another standard, the CM requests the required documentation from the contractor at the earliest point in the project. If there are plans to use an independent commissioning agent (CA), the CM should compile all related documentation throughout the life of the project, but especially during the construction phase. If the owner hires a CA, the CM ensures that the CA provides the proper paperwork in a timely fashion.

SUSTAINABILITY RFI'S OR USGBC CREDIT INTERPRETATION REQUESTS

When a project strives to achieve specific sustainable goals (or in the case of USGBC registered LEED, "to be certified projects"), requests for additional information may require credit interpretations. The pre-construction conference should discuss and agree to a system/procedure to vet these requests. The traditional RFI approach may be appropriate depending on the complexity of the sustainable applications.

8.5   Post-Construction Phase

GBI, LEED, OR OTHER APPLICATION PROCESS

The CM must ensure that the contractors provided all documentation necessary for certification and that the contract requires. The CM also ensures that both the CM and contractor fulfilled all assigned responsibilities. The project's designated agent submits the Green Globes, LEED, or other application. This could be the CM, contractor, designer, or the project's sustainability champion.

GBI, LEED, OR OTHER REVIEW PROCESS

After they receive the preliminary Green Globes/LEED/other review document that notes the credit achievement anticipated, pending, or denied, the designated agent meets with the designer, contractor, and owner to review the comments with the team and establish an action plan to resolve all open issues.

TRAINING SESSIONS

If the project installed specific sustainability elements, the contract documents should specify appropriate training. This training should finish before closeout and use the delivered O&M manuals. The CM confirms that the appropriate facilities management personnel, as well as the owner, have access to the training. The training should include an introduction that repeats the project's sustainable goals and objectives.

FINAL OWNER SIGN-OFF

The CM should only recommend final owner sign-off once all the project sustainability plan and construction document requirements are complete and verified.

Notes

Notes

CHAPTER 9

Technology Management

9.1 Introduction

Construction technology generally refers to the systems, tools, equipment, and software used to organize and manipulate data, materials, and other resources to complete a capital construction project. Technology integration on a project may include automated or semi-automated methods to complete specific project tasks in a way that improves quality, cost, time, or risk.

Technology should provide innovative solutions, simplify tasks, and improve project delivery. Technology and innovative thought leadership can add value to the owner to save time, increase predictable results, and improve performance, productivity, and collaboration.

The CM must establish themselves as a thought leader and advise the owner on technology. The CM does not need to be an expert on technology, but they should understand what current technology options are available, who the experts are that can answer questions, and anticipate new technology. A CM must also understand technology's ethical implications (i.e., the ways technology can be good or bad).

This chapter provides a brief overview of the technology topics that are specific to the CM's role. This section is not comprehensive of all construction technology, as many technologies exist to complete a capital construction project that are specific to the designer, builder, or other stakeholders. It is the CM's responsibility to be aware of and understand those technologies when appropriate to the project, but they are beyond this chapter's scope.

9.2 Key Concepts and Tools

This section provides a summary of some important CM technology topics that may apply throughout all project phases.

ARTIFICIAL INTELLIGENCE (AI)

AI applies computer algorithms to replicate actions that humans perform. Many industry experts also use the term "machine learning" to refer to AI concepts. AI software "learns" from the data it receives to attempt to make more accurate decisions and predictions about project cost, schedule, risk, etc. However, AI is only as good as the inputs it receives and the CM who interprets the output.

Bad or inefficient data will not produce accurate or reliable AI solutions. Data collection in the construction industry usually lags behind other industries, so historical information may be necessary to best use AI. Finding historical data may be too demanding for smaller projects but should be easier for larger projects and organizations.

The CM's responsibility is to understand the project's scope to advise the owner on how to best use AI. AI can reduce risk, but the CM must explain to the owner any limitations and risks AI may create. For example, AI may be able to calculate a zero-float schedule but not be able to predict weather impacts. AI may also be able to identify claims that a human could not, which creates potential claims risks. The CM must confirm that all contract documents reflect how the owner wishes to use AI. The owner may need to prepare for unique or challenging claims, train staff to use AI, and ensure that contractors recognize that AI will highlight poor management practices.

AUGMENTED REALITY (AR)/VIRTUAL REALITY (VR)

AR is an interactive tool that overlays digital information onto real-world objects, whereas VR fully immerses a user in a digital environment. Humans can use multiple tools, mediums, and methods to view AR/VR data, including tablets and headsets. On a project site, users may receive data based on their physical location or proximity to an object. For example, a worker on a project site using AR may be able to point a camera at a wall and instantly see an overlay on a screen that shows the utilities or equipment positioned behind the wall.

AR/VR can increase project efficiency and safety but is only as reliable as the data it is given. The CM's role is to evaluate the project's information needs and advise the owner on how to best use AR/VR.

BUILDING INFORMATION MODELING (BIM)

BIM is a method to create a digital representation of the physical and functional characteristics of a facility that a project team can virtually analyze, document, and assess, then revise iteratively throughout the design and construction process. Throughout the facility's lifetime, the model serves as a shared knowledge resource that forms a reliable basis for decisions during the facility's lifecycle from inception through design to construction, use/occupancy, operations, renovation, and eventual demolition.

BIM provides data and context, which allows a project team to produce drawings faster as well as help collaboration, increase efficiency, reduce risk, and improve safety. A BIM model helps the project team analyze and communicate the construction process in a virtual environment, including the sequence of work, means and methods, logistics, and documentation of as-built conditions.

BIM uses a digital database (or common data environment) to define, store, and analyze facility characteristics. This makes it possible to use BIM for qualitative and quantitative analyses. This application of scientific analytic principles and processes to reveal the properties and state of the project is an example of engineering analysis.

History of BIM

For many years, the industry often used the term "BIM" to refer to all technological innovations, with the expectation that BIM would improve collaboration, cost-effectiveness, productivity, and information accessibility because there would be one data source. BIM's process to convert paper models to computer-aided design (CAD) models transformed the construction industry, but BIM also presented challenges with adoption, integration, cost, and risk of ownership.

BIM gradually evolved to where the CM can now access virtual models on the jobsite to coordinate the installation of a facility's systems. At first, CAD technology made the design process more efficient, but parts of the industry resisted adoption. Then, the industry began to use federated models that combine the architectural model, structural model, and mechanical, electrical, and plumbing (MEP) model. The industry also adopted operations models for O&M. These models are now accessible in the field with mobile technology.

Clash Detection

Clash detection is a method to check for interferences by searching for intersecting volumes. This application provides the opportunity to not only clash a single model but combine and clash multiple models from disparate sources in a common environment.

BIM Dimensions

A BIM model includes multiple dimensions that may include the following:

» **3D Parametric Modeling:** A digital representation of physical and functional characteristics of a facility that provides a better design environment than 2D CAD. 3D modeling applications can capture design intent parametrically. This facilitates model creation and editing, which reduces the likelihood of coordination errors. BIM 3D environments can export traditional 2D documents, therefore making the BIM 3D environment the source of official 2D drawing documentation.

» **4D Scheduling:** A 4D scheduling application dynamically links the project CPM schedule activities to 3D objects in the BIM. This allows for a graphically rich and animated representation of the planned construction sequence over time. 4D schedules are a tool for phasing, coordinating, and communicating planned work to a variety of audiences, including project stakeholders and those solely responsible for executing the work. These schedules also support simulated what-if scenarios.

» **5D Cost Estimating:** Every BIM element is attributed to what it will represent in terms of resources and respective costs. This allows a parametric and dynamic quantity takeoff for bills of materials, resulting in a more accurate estimate and allows the estimators to spend less time on the quantity take-off and more time performing the cost estimate analysis.

» **6D Sustainability:** A 6D application applies sustainability and energy efficiency elements to the model, which provides an estimate of the facility's energy costs, environmental impact, pollution risks, etc.

» **7D Facility Management:** The model applies facility management elements, which allows a more accurate estimate of the owner's operation and maintenance costs over the facility's entire lifecycle.

- » **8D Safety:** An 8D application provides safety information. This dimension's safety model includes operators' risks and helps to prevent critical hazardous scenarios.
- » **9D Lean Construction:** This dimension applies lean construction elements to the model, which may benefit the use of automated machinery on the project site, pre-fabrication of building materials, etc.

Models may combine many BIM dimensions but still be in the early conceptual stages (and missing details).

Level of Development (LOD)

A BIM model's level of development (LOD) refers to the effort that the project team spends developing a BIM model's detail, which may determine the model's reliability. As a BIM model's LOD increases, the ease and efficiency with which the structure can be built also increases.

The CM must understand the following LOD levels[2]:

- » **LOD 100:** A conceptual model that derives information from other model elements
- » **LOD 200:** Schematic layout with approximate size, shape, and location
- » **LOD 300:** Modeled as design-specified size, shape, spacing, and location of equipment
- » **LOD 350:** Modeled as actual size, shape, spacing with location and connections of equipment
- » **LOD 400:** Supplementary components added to the model required for fabrication and field installation

BIM Integrator

Certain project delivery methods require a project team member to serve as the BIM integrator. The BIM integrator could be the CM, an architect/engineer, builder, or independent party. The BIM integrator's responsibilities include:

- » Ensure a smooth transition of the model from the design to the construction phase.
- » Always maintain a central model and incorporate the latest available information from multiple project participants.
- » Bring new project team members (sub-contractors, vendors, etc.) up to speed on the BIM project objectives and current model status.
- » Ensure a complete and thorough transition of the model from the construction phase to the owner.
- » In all the project phases, verify that the model meets the owner's BIM requirements and the project's BIM specifications.
- » Assure interoperability between models on those projects that require a multiple model approach.

Virtual Design and Construction (VDC)

VDC uses data to plan a structure's *physical* construction process, whereas BIM uses data to build *virtual* models of a structure. Many methods exist to conduct VDC, but BIM is the most common.

Transitioning the BIM Model to the Owner

The owner benefits at the project's end when the project team transitions a BIM model to the owner for facility management. The model's specifications depend on the owner's facility management systems, current operations, and maintenance processes and procedures. The facility's operations office is responsible for mastering the as-built and facility management model.

The CM helps the owner's facility management team define what they will need from the model and how to format the information for future use. The CM also manages the proper training for the owners and the facility operators.

BUSINESS INTELLIGENCE (BI)

BI (also known as data mining) is the process of transforming raw data into actionable data. It is a systematic approach to manage extremely large volumes of data stored in databases or data warehouses. BI tools normalize and correlate data, identify outliers and missing data, and find patterns using advanced algorithms and standardized methods. Modern BI tools can also analyze both structured and unstructured data.

Source data must first exist in a digital format in a single platform. Raw data may exist in hard copy or in business silos with different units of measurement, workplace cultures, and other conditions. Human information managers may first need to collect, digitize, and format the source data in a consolidated platform before BI tools can analyze it. This process to organize and define the data may involve an algorithm that sorts the information to detect outliers or missing data. This is known as "scrubbing" or "normalizing" source data.

BI tools must either be a part of the MIS or at least interface with it. (See MIS in **Chapter 2: Project Management** and **Chapter 11: Program Management**.)

In the construction industry, BI can gather and transform quantitative data into actionable information to help project or program delivery. BI tools can help CMs and owners improve operational efficiency, deliver faster and more accurate reporting, and make more well-informed decisions.

Many BI tools analyze and present information in a visual, interactive "dashboard." These dashboards show real-time information and allow the CM (or other users) to track multiple performance indicators across a project or program. Modern BI tools also allow users to combine different data sets or sources as well as run searches to draw conclusions. Data analysis may be descriptive (show what is happening), predictive (indicate what might happen), or prescriptive (recommend actions based on what might happen).

When using BI tools, it is the CM's responsibility to advise the owner on the relevant information for their project or organization and to maximize actionable knowledge. The CM does not need to be a BI expert but should understand what tools are appropriate, what data is available, and how to best interpret/present that data.

Clients often hire CMs for competencies that the client may not have, so the CM must discuss BI's benefits with the owner and guide them to deploy the most appropriate tool. The CM must also know what data is important (and what is not important) and relay that to the relevant database programmers to ensure that the project team correctly interprets scrubbed data. The CM should also know who has access to the data and make sure appropriate stakeholders receive only the information they need.

CYBERSECURITY

Cybersecurity is a practice to allow project stakeholders to access appropriate information from digital systems and devices while also protecting that data from unauthorized persons/entities.

The CM's cybersecurity role is to understand the owner's information security requirements and ensure that the project team uses appropriate cybersecurity tools. For example, a public owner may require compliance with the U.S. Department of Defense's Cybersecurity Maturity Model Certification (CMMC), Federal Risk and Authorization Management Program (FedRAMP), and the Federal Information Security Management Act (FISMA).

Protecting information is critical to project success, but avoiding new digital tools because of potential cyber threats could also limit successful outcomes. The CM must balance security and the ability to share information among stakeholders.

DATA MANAGEMENT

Data management is a clear and secure process to create, store, share, monitor, and process data. Data comes in many forms on a construction project, including cost, schedule, risk, safety, quality, and communications data. The CM ensures that the project team identifies subject matter experts to evaluate data and data sources to maintain the integrity and useability of project data.

DIGITAL TWIN

A digital twin is a virtual model linked to physical elements, components, and processes on the actual construction site for the full project lifecycle. Digital twins use real-time and historical data, which can help the project team make decisions and simulate future outcomes. The project team manages the digital twin throughout the project in a virtual environment that receives regular updates from other reality capture tools that capture and assemble this data.

The CM's responsibility is to explain to the owner how digital twin technology can reduce risk. The CM must also understand new opportunities to collect real-time data from the jobsite. New sensors and wireless internet connections allow project teams to consume information and make decisions faster.

ETHICS

All technology can be used for good or bad, so the CM must help establish clear guidelines and a strong workplace culture that considers technology's full impact. For example, BI tools, drones/unmanned aerial vehicles (UAVs), and automated systems can improve efficiency but also present potential privacy and safety concerns.

The CM must realize that their technology decisions impact all levels within the industry. The CM should help the project team implement checks and balances. A CM must also encourage the owner to communicate with their employees about new technologies and consider how these tools might be misused.

PHOTOGRAMMETRY

Photogrammetry is a process that uses overlapping photographs of an object or area and converts them into 2D or 3D models. A variety of devices and methods can collect photogrammetric data, including 360-degree cameras, wearables, drones/UAVs, SONAR, RADAR, and LiDAR. Good data can help the project team make better decisions to reduce costs, avoid delays, and improve safety. It is the CM's responsibility to understand what photogrammetric tools are appropriate to the project and advise the owner.

RETURN ON INVESTMENT (ROI)

ROI is a performance measure used to evaluate the efficiency of an investment. A CM should view technology as an investment instead of a cost and realize that technology can deliver quantifiable benefits. The CM must also help the project team define their ROI expectations.

When considering a new technology, the CM has a standard of care to select technology that enhances a project's ROI. The CM should know how a technology improves performance, simplifies tasks, increases delivery, etc. To accomplish this, the CM must understand the project as well as their own organization and the owner's comfort with adopting new technology. The CM should also recognize that sometimes the best solution for a project is not a new technology.

SYSTEMS INTEGRATION

There are many technologies that can make project delivery more successful, but technology that the project team does not properly manage creates inefficiencies, drains resources, and increases project costs. As a system becomes more complex, the risk grows that it will isolate or duplicate data in silos. This creates inefficiencies that may include the following:

» Manual data re-entry
» Duplication of business functions
» Reliance on paper to duplicate and exchange data

Systems integration provides a project team with a "single point of truth" to efficiently share data, collaborate, and make decisions. This ability to exchange information seamlessly reduces the number of data entry points and allows stakeholders to receive data specific to their needs. This means that software from different manufacturers exchange information and work together for project success. This interoperability speeds up project delivery, reduces infrastructure vulnerability, decreases supply-chain costs, and improves value to the owner.

Common software tools that project teams may choose to integrate include the following:

- » MIS
- » BIM software
- » Geospatial information software
- » Asset management software
- » Reporting and dashboarding software
- » Financial software
- » Scheduling software
- » Space planning

The CM's responsibility is to advise the owner on the most appropriate system integration options for the project or program. Organizations that do not integrate systems are less efficient, but owners and project teams may choose not to integrate systems or only partially integrate systems due to the cost, security risks, or control issues associated with integration. The CM must carefully evaluate all risks to make the best recommendation, recognizing that full integration and interoperability may not always be in the owner's best interest.

TECHNOLOGY CHARTER

The CM applies the latest technology and trends to solve problems, increase project efficiency, and add value to their clients and organizations. A technology charter helps the CM guide these processes.

An organization should create a technology charter to serve as a guide to:

- » Define a process for technology application, evaluation, and adoption while considering the ideal final output, team capabilities, and available resources.
- » Define how the organization interacts with technology, both in-house and with its clients.
- » Establish rules for data access and security.
- » Form the organizational structure to manage and implement new technology adoption.
- » Adopt a process to define cost/benefit and ROI for new applications.

5G

5G is the 5th generation of wireless communication standards and is at least ten times faster than 4G LTE. 5G has the speed to process data-intensive BIM models remotely over wireless connections, reducing the weight, size, and computing power needed in handheld or wearable devices. However, remote locations often do not have the latest generation or strong wireless connectivity. The CM's role is to understand the wireless coverage that is available on the jobsite and help the project team use it efficiently.

9.3   Pre-Design Phase

The pre-design phase's goal is for the owner to clearly establish technology's role in the scope of work, phases of implementation, team responsibilities, and expected outcome. The CM must look for opportunities to use technology that will increase the project's efficiency and add value. The CM educates the owner on the use of technology and promotes its appropriate use. The owner must understand any implications that might affect the project as well as the shortcomings of any of the technology used on the project.

The CM helps the owner to establish the Condition of Satisfaction (COS). The COS should be tangible and part of the project's technology goals and objectives. BIM expectations and the BIM team qualifications are set as early as possible to ensure alignment of the expectations with the BIM roles and responsibilities among project stakeholders. The CM helps the owner define common terminology and expectations in all contracts so that all project stakeholders are referring to the same technology consistently throughout the project.

PROJECT MANAGEMENT PLAN (PMP)

The CM develops the PMP, which addresses the anticipated tools and technology needed throughout all project phases. If the project uses BIM, the PMP either establishes the BIM modeling criteria or refers to it as a separate document called the BIM project execution plan. The BIM procedures explain the project's BIM standards, including distribution and access protocols. The design contract also includes these standards.

SELECTING THE DESIGN TEAM

The CM advertises the project to the design community and seeks design teams to submit proposals. If the PMP requires BIM, the CM includes BIM experience in the design team selection criteria listed in the request for qualifications (RFQ). During the RFQ review and interview process, the owner and CM should evaluate the BIM capabilities of the design teams with respect to how important BIM is to the project.

The CM works with the owner's legal counsel to develop the design team contract, which includes appropriate language for technology's use on the project. The contract must address:

» Pay application processing and review.

» Tools and methods for as-built documentation (such as photography and laser scanning).

» Documentation procedures so that the owner has continued access to design documents after project closeout.

» Standards for project record communications, including email, video conferencing, etc.

» Protocols for document control and distribution (such as the use of electronic information systems) for issue logs, meeting minutes, progress reports, etc. For BIM projects, these protocols must define procedures for accessing and manipulating BIM model(s).

If the project uses BIM, the contract language should include BIM requirements. The contract must address the format of the BIM model, including the level of detail and allowable use of 2D detailing. This may also include how the design team should develop and share the BIM model with other project team members.

TECHNOLOGY AND PROJECT DELIVERY METHODS

The CM must recognize that technology's use varies depending on what project delivery method the owner chooses. In the design-bid-build method, the project team is more likely to struggle to integrate new technologies after a project begins because contracts are less collaborative and integration becomes more expensive. Technology is easier to integrate with other delivery methods, such as CM at-risk and design-build.

9.4   Design Phase

For projects that use BIM, the CM conducts a BIM kickoff meeting to explain and build consensus for the project's BIM standards and implementation procedures that the contract documents established in the pre-design phase.

DESIGN DOCUMENT REVIEW

Periodic design review meetings must address and monitor compliance with established BIM standards. The CM and designer (or design-build team) must review design milestone submittals (such as schematic, design development, construction documents) for compliance with established BIM standards.

The BIM model helps the project team comply with design criteria and perform group design reviews. The BIM model allows the team to visualize the spaces and functions, optimize the design, and make decisions. The CM takes full advantage of the visualization benefits of the BIM model so that the owner, user groups, and stakeholders can see the project virtually and minimize the potential for changes after construction. This should include clash detection and coordination among all design disciplines.

DOCUMENT CONTROL

The CM (or BIM integrator) ensures that the project team follows the document distribution and control protocols established in the pre-design phase. If any revisions to the document control protocols are necessary, the CM also updates the BIM procedures.

PUBLIC RELATIONS

The CM helps the owner communicate project details to the community and other public stakeholders. The CM may use the BIM model, phasing, and 4D simulation as part of these communications.

COST CONTROL

The project team may use AI to identify cost variances and opportunities to increase design efficiency. The CM ensures that AI's use follows the contract specifications, ensures that all project team members understand AI's role, and advises the owner regarding any potential claims.

The CM tries to maximize model-based budgeting and estimating if required by the project's BIM objectives. If the design must fully utilize BIM processes, the CM collaborates with the design team to define model development criteria and enable model-based estimating. The cost structures develop earlier than in a conventional project to benefit most from the model. Options analysis and VE use the model-based budget and estimate, including in any needed exercises to modify the design to match the budget.

9.5   Procurement Phase

The CM must remember during procurement that each project delivery method uses technology differently. For example, technology integration and collaboration are usually most difficult in the design-bid-build method. The CM must tailor the procurement process to the specific delivery method and owner's requirements, as necessary.

BID DOCUMENTS

The CM must encourage the owner and designer to formally include any relevant technology documentation (such as the BIM models) in the procurement documents. This approach helps bidders to better understand the project. If the owner and designer choose not to formally include these documents, the CM should recommend their use as reference documents.

PROJECT MARKETING

The CM markets the project and generates interest from entities that understand and are qualified to meet the project's technological requirements.

PRE-BID OR PRE-PROPOSAL MEETING

The CM highlights and explains the project's technology requirements to prospective bidders. The CM uses the BIM model to explain the project and generate comments or questions from potential bidders.

CONTRACTS/AGREEMENTS

The contract documents must include the owner's technology requirements, which the PMP usually establishes.

When the PMP requires full BIM implementation, the CM verifies that the contract documents require project participants to update and revise the model and all parts, sub-models, and databases to reflect as-built conditions. The contract documents should require linking the documented models and databases as well as submitting them at the end of the project. The contracts must include training on how to access information from the updated BIM model.

SELECTION OF CONTRACTOR(S): DESIGN-BID-BUILD, CM AT-RISK, OR DESIGN-BUILD

In the case of a design-bid-build process, the CM uses the prequalification process and includes experience with the project's technological requirements as one of the selection factors. After the owner and CM evaluate the bids, the owner and CM hold a pre-award conference with the apparent low or best value bidder. The CM verifies that the contractor's capabilities comply with the project's requirements as stated in the contract documents.

For CM at-risk or design-build, the selection process often includes a review of written proposals and interview(s). The CM reviews the proposals for compliance with the project's technological requirements. In the interviews, the CM ensures that the entities clearly articulate their technology approach and capabilities. The CM also ensures that the owner considers these factors in the selection.

9.6   Construction Phase

The CM encourages proactive stakeholder participation. The CM ensures that the contract language and scope of work clearly define the technology responsibilities for each stakeholder. This includes:

» Owner/operator
» Designer
» Contractor and subcontractors
» Suppliers
» Equipment manufacturers
» System integrators
» Select third parties, such as building official(s), local utility companies, insurers, and sureties

If using BIM, the CM (or the BIM integrator) and the construction team use the document control protocol established earlier in the project to transition the BIM model to the construction phase. At this point, BIM is also known as VDC.

The CM ensures that the project team updates the model throughout the construction phase and that the model evolves into an as-built model for record purposes (if required by the owner). The builder may start its own model rather than build upon the designer's model. Regardless of the approach, the CM ensures that contract language clearly explains which entity is responsible for updating the model as an as-built document and on the desired level of detail.

The CM also monitors compliance to verify that the owner receives a proper as-built model at the end of construction, in accordance with the contract requirements.

ON-SITE COORDINATION

The CM encourages the project team to use technology to address problems encountered in the field. The CM's role on a BIM project is to ensure and encourage the full use of the BIM tool in coordination and issue resolution. Field personnel should also use connected mobile devices to coordinate construction and extend technology's impact. To facilitate this capability on projects of appropriate size and complexity, an on-site model and a designated BIM integrator should be available to monitor and update the model as the project moves forward.

The contractor, CM at-risk, or design-builder is responsible for project coordination throughout construction. Regardless of the project delivery method, the contract should obligate the builder to use the model to ensure project coordination. This includes revising the model based on existing conditions, incorporating information from subcontractors' shop drawing submittals, and clash detection.

TIME MANAGEMENT

The CM encourages the builder to use the 4D model for time management. It is prudent for the CM to develop a project-specific 4D model using BIM. The construction schedule is tied to the model to allow visualization of deviations from planned sequences and durations. This practice is part of the periodic progress review process. To accomplish this, the CM establishes the protocol through the contract documents or procedures manual.

RFIS, SUBMITTALS, AND SHOP DRAWINGS

The team should use an effective MIS to establish workflows, alerts, and queues to automate the flow of RFIs, submittals, and shop drawings.

The CM encourages the project team to use the model to produce shop drawings. The design team can review the model the builder submits. If required, these requirements must be defined in the PMP, stated in the designer's and builder's (or design-builder's) contract documents, and project procedures. The use of the model for RFI review helps the design team visualize the conditions related to the RFI. The CM needs to verify that stakeholders support this process to maximize the chances of success.

CHANGE ORDERS

When reviewing and pricing change orders, a BIM model helps the CM to visualize the change. The builder is usually responsible for documenting the change orders on the model, but the contract documents must clearly explain who holds this responsibility. The CM verifies that the model includes the change orders as well as the posting of the changes to the as-built documents.

An effective MIS also helps with workflows, alerts, and queues to manage change orders.

OWNER-PURCHASED MATERIALS AND EQUIPMENT

If the owner supplies any additional components, materials, or equipment, the builder or BIM integrator updates the model to include the owner-purchased designation. The project team can extract quantities and SOV for the materials from the BIM model for an accurate count and to save time.

9.7 Post-Construction Phase

The CM ensures that the handover to the owner satisfies the owner's expectations for the facility's future use. The CM recognizes that the owner may not understand what tools and data are available, so the CM advises the owner on potential tools, their ROIs, and how to prioritize them. If using BIM, the CM works closely with the project team and the owner's facility management team to define what the facility management team needs from the model for future use.

The commissioning agent (CA) may have its own digital platform for tracking commissioning data, so the CM verifies that the owner's O&M system incorporates the CA's data. This may include inputting appropriate data into the BIM/VDC models for transition to the owner.

At a minimum, the CM transitions the model to the owner as an as-built model. This provides facility management benefits to the owner, such as space planning for occupant assignment, furniture, equipment inventory, etc. The CM verifies that the as-built model links to copies of the final permits, schedules of spare parts (and related warranties), and asset/facilities management records for the owner's use.

The CM also ensures that the owner's O&M personnel receive training on the BIM/VDC model and the facility's systems, as required in the contract documents. The CM also facilitates and verifies that the as-built model links to training documentation and operating procedures for the owner's O&M staff.

[2]*More information about levels of development is available in the American Institute of Architects (AIA) contract documents at* **https://www.aiacontracts.org** *and on the United States BIMForum website at* **https://bimforum.org/LOD/**.

Notes

CHAPTER 10

Risk Management

10.1 Introduction

> **Risk (n.) A source of danger; the possibility of suffering harm or loss.**

> **Contract (n.) A tool for allocating risk to the party best able to manage it.**

In the context of design and construction, risk management is the process to methodically address risk and to reduce the impact of risk events on a project or program in all development phases. The opposite of risk is opportunity, which can potentially improve quality and reduce overall project/program cost and schedule.

Risk is part of major capital construction projects, so this chapter intends to provide the CM with a standard guide to implement project risk management. Risk management is part of any business, including that of the owner and CM. Risk management includes contract administration topics such as insurance requirements, waivers, bonds, liquidated damages, claims, and indemnity provisions.

Risk management's goal is to provide a system to identify risks and opportunities early on a construction project or program as well as track and manage them throughout the project. Although some risk events are unpredictable, certain actions and decisions during a project's planning stages can create other risks which are predictable. This chapter focuses on how to plan mitigation of risk consequences, such as potential losses, damages, loss of opportunities, or any other undesirable events.

Some owners may rely on the CM for risk management services more than others. The CM reviews project scope, cost, and schedule to identify risks and opportunities to manage throughout the project. The CM also reviews project contracts for potential risks and liabilities, determines the potential impact of contract clauses, and develops a plan to address these potential impacts. This does not replace the role of legal counsel. An owner may transfer risks to a third party, mitigate them with project insurance, or minimize or eliminate them with design and engineering.

10.2 Risk Management Planning

Risk management planning begins early in project development. Effective project development on large and complex projects often requires participants to apply risk management processes during the pre-design and design phases.

All construction project plans are based on estimates with uncertainty. With uncertainty, there is also the risk of unfavorable consequences, which are often more severe on larger or more complex projects.

The best way to address uncertainty and the associated risk consequences is to develop and implement a risk management process as part of the construction management process. A structured risk management methodology is a key project management process that should receive the same level of attention as budget control, scheduling, decision-making, and claims avoidance. Risk management should be a continuous, integrated project management process on projects.

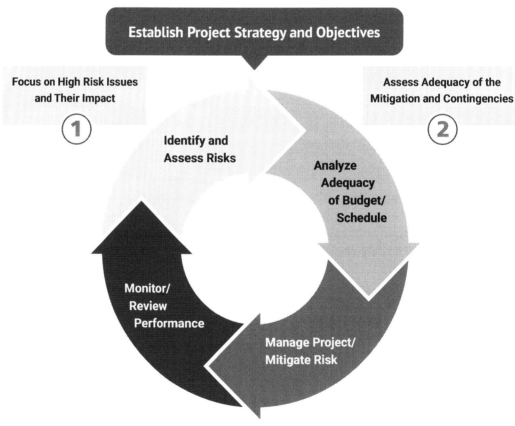

An iterative and continuous process for managing risk as it changes and shifts.

Figure 1: Continuous risk strategy and management—an iterative and continuous process for managing risk as it changes and shifts

Figure 1 illustrates the overall objectives of a strategic risk management process. The first risk management step is to acknowledge that it is impossible to eliminate the potential for risk consequences, but they can be mitigated.

Major capital construction projects often face many types of risk events, such as adverse weather, differing site conditions, required or desired scope changes, unavailability of specific types of resources, unanticipated environmental factors, or community pressures. The adverse effects associated with these events normally result in increased cost, re-sequencing of construction activities, and delays that might interfere with successful project delivery.

The risk management process should start at the project's beginning with the development of a design and construction risk management plan, which details the processes planned for assessing, mitigating, and managing the potential risks. The plan should contain a statement of purpose for the risk management process and the overall project performance objectives.

The plan also summarizes key definitions of risk terminology, establishes program and process policies, and identifies each stage of the process. The plan documents the project's risk identification and mitigation methods, which guides the project team's overall understanding of the risk management processes and helps create a personal connection and commitment to use the risk management methodology.

The risk management plan generally includes the following major steps:

» Risk identification

» Risk analysis

» Risk management

The project team should hold risk management meetings during each of the five phases of project/program development (pre-design, design, procurement, construction, post-construction) to identify and prioritize the manageable risks within each phase. The meetings categorize risks as internal (within the project team's control) or external (outside the project team's control).

The CM follows the risk management plan's implementation steps during each project phase. The CM should consider the following in each phase and include the following participants at a minimum in the risk meetings:

1. **Pre-design:** Review the design concepts and studies, potential external challenges or deterrents to the project, funding, schedule, community impact, etc. The review should include the CM, owner, designers, and project stakeholders.

2. **Design:** Review the construction plans and specifications, proposed schedule, estimated costs, utility relocations and coordination, environmental mitigation, land purchases or issues, permitting, constraints, access, etc. Before advertising for bids, review construction contract language with special emphasis on the appropriate allocation or mitigation of identified risk items and the potential impact on scope, cost, and schedule. The review should include the CM, owner, designers, and construction representatives, if possible.

3. **Procurement:** Review questions from bidders for possible unidentified issues or risks, adequacy of the number of bidders, and necessary addenda. The review should include the CM, owner, contractor, technical personnel who are experts on the issues, and project stakeholders.

4. **Construction:** Review previously identified risks throughout construction to ensure they are appropriately managed, review unforeseen conditions or other risks not previously identified, and review potential construction change issues affecting scope, cost, and schedule. The review should include the CM, owner, designer, contractor, and representatives with input to critical construction issues.

5. **Post-construction:** Review warranties, maintenance and operations plan, any outstanding construction items, and any potential claims. The review should include the CM, owner, O&M personnel, and contractor representative (if necessary).

The following sections in this chapter describe the services the CM typically provides a client for the major risk management plan implementation steps. The *CMAA Risk Management Guidelines* provide additional recommended details to carry out these steps.

10.3   Risk Identification

Risk identification is the process of evaluating the project to be constructed and recognizing risks (typically related to scope, cost, and schedule) that could impact the project.

Many risk managers, consultants, owners, and insurance companies have lists, surveys, audit forms, and other means of collecting and documenting the risks on typical projects. The PM should develop a risk register to identify and monitor all the risks associated with the program. Some important items in risk identification include:

Strategic Risk Processes	
Employing risk management processes to help attain and meet expectations	
SUCCESSFUL PROJECT	**ADDED BENEFITS**
✓ Maximize opportunities ✓ Minimize risk impacts	✓ Cost-effectiveness ✓ Schedule control ✓ Contingency management

Figure 2: Overall strategy of the risk management program

» **Realistic project assumptions:** Do not allow idealistic interpretations of the project assumptions or promote the idea that all will go according to plan.

» **Gather expert judgments:** Collect a variety of expert judgments which support unbiased assessments and analysis.

» **Clearly understand risk elements and their impacts:** In the early phases of project planning and development, clearly understand each risk element and its potential impacts.

» **View project realistically, not idealistically:** For an effective risk management strategy, the project's expected cost and schedule results must be objective and realistic.

The CM helps organize teams to assist in identifying risk as early as possible on a program, with the first meetings in the pre-design phase. Each project phase should hold continued meetings to identify, analyze, and manage risks.

Figure 2 illustrates the importance of the strategic risk process and risk identification to ultimately minimize the impact of risks and maximize any identified opportunities.

10.4   Risk Analysis

The identification and logging of the risks and opportunities is only the beginning of the risk management process. After identification, an analysis of a project's risks and opportunities can provide the project team and stakeholders with a structured assessment of the risk's potential to impact the project. This allows the team to focus on those risks considered to have the greatest potential project impact that also have the chance of occurrence. An example of the qualitative portion of this evaluation is scoring the severity versus the likelihood of an event.

Risk Event Status

SEVERITY	LIKELIHOOD				
	Minor	Unlikely	Possible	Likely	Almost Certain
Critical	Serious	Major	Major	Critical	Critical
Major	Moderate	Serious	Major	Major	Critical
Serious	Moderate	Moderate	Serious	Serious	Major
Moderate	Moderate	Moderate	Moderate	Serious	Serious
Minor	Minor	Minor	Moderate	Moderate	Serious

Figure 3: Risk evaluation scoring criteria

Figure 3 is based on input from the project team most familiar with the risk potential. This method evaluates (or scores) risks based on the likelihood that the risk will occur and the severity of the project impact should it occur.

Note that no figures are estimated in this qualitative review, but the matrix of likelihood and severity allows the project team to categorize risk from "critical" to "minor." This guide helps to identify where to devote time to project risks. When the CM moves the team into the quantitative review, the team estimates figures for severity and percentages for likelihood to better define potential risk impacts.

The CM must ensure that after the project team identifies all the risks that they also analyze them to determine their potential impact on the project. The participants should also determine which project team members should follow up on action items related to each risk. These assignments then become part of the risk management plan.

Important points of the risk analysis include:

» **Assess and analyze risks' impacts:** Complete the evaluation and analysis of risks to determine the impacts they will have on the project's goals and objectives.
» **Complete mitigation and contingency plans:** Fully develop mitigation and contingency plans that are appropriate to the degree of impact for the identified risks.
» **Synthesize the risks:** Synthesize all construction risks and determine the total cumulative effects.

10.5   Risk Management Process

After identifying and assessing risks and opportunities, the knowledge and information gathered help to effectively manage them. The CM ensures that all project phases follow a structured process to ensure that the project team manages risks and opportunities, avoiding unnecessary risk impacts and realizing potential opportunities. The following are four essential components of the risk management process.

COMMUNICATION AND REPORTING

The CM holds project team meetings that use the project risk database (which includes all the risks and opportunities identified). The CM communicates the risks/opportunities and collects feedback, updates, and other related information. Internal project personnel who should be aware and are in the best position to mitigate the risks or achieve an opportunity receive reports.

TRACKING

With each update from the project risk meetings, the project team provides input to help track and adjust risks/opportunities. The project may retire risks/opportunities if the project team believes there is no longer a potential project impact. New items may also join the list as they become known. Tracking updates and communication must happen consistently to maintain focus on the project team's priorities.

MITIGATION

As the project team identifies risks, the team should assign primary responsibility for the risk to a team member. This entity or individual has the most opportunity to mitigate the risk and minimize any impact on the project. The assignee must provide a risk mitigation plan. This plan is a set of action items with responsibilities and required dates, with the intent that those responsible for these actions will provide the best possibility to mitigate the risk to reduce the impact.

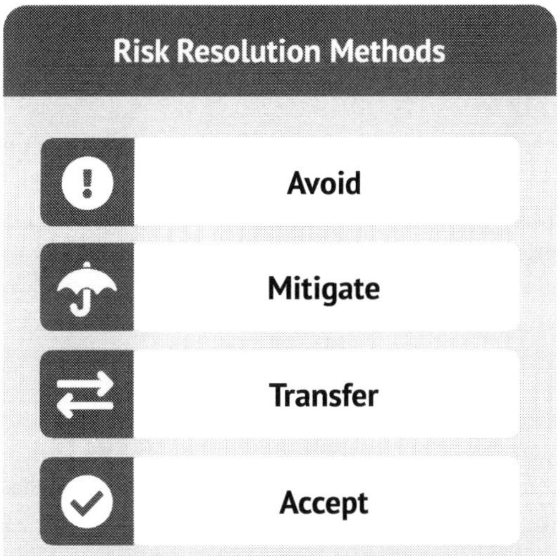

RESOLUTION

Project risks resolve as the mitigation plan executes, action items finish, and project decisions are made. A project can avoid (eliminate), mitigate, transfer (defer), or accept risks (with an impact on the project). As risks come to a resolution, updates to the risk data should include the results, notes related to the resolution, and any lessons learned related to the risks.

Risk Resolution Methods

- **!** Avoid
- **☂** Mitigate
- **⇄** Transfer
- **✓** Accept

Figure 4: Risk resolution methods

Figure 5: Risk management cycle

Figure 5 documents the flow from the risk management planning to risk identification and risk analysis, before ending with a resolution where the risk is avoided, mitigated, transferred, or accepted, with an ultimate assessed impact on the project. The risk log thoroughly documents this risk management process to work with the other project control tools, such as budget and schedule management as well as reporting and communications. The log may also help share lessons learned and serve as a reference for future similar projects.

10.6   Continuous Evaluation of Risk Effects

Any project can expect identified risks to grow and present many potential impacts. As a capital project transitions into the procurement and construction phases, risks can change. Many risks outside of the project team's control have the potential to cause impacts if not continually monitored.

From the beginning, the owner's construction management process should have an ongoing integrated process for risk management based on sound basic principles. Risk management should not be an independent function. The CM, on behalf of the owner, should have a process to implement new mitigation strategies and options as project conditions change.

A continuous integrated risk management process will help reduce the potential for unidentified negative impacts, improve the CM's continuous efforts to obtain consensus, promote collaboration, and maintain a steady focus on the project's constraints and objectives.

10.7   Conclusion

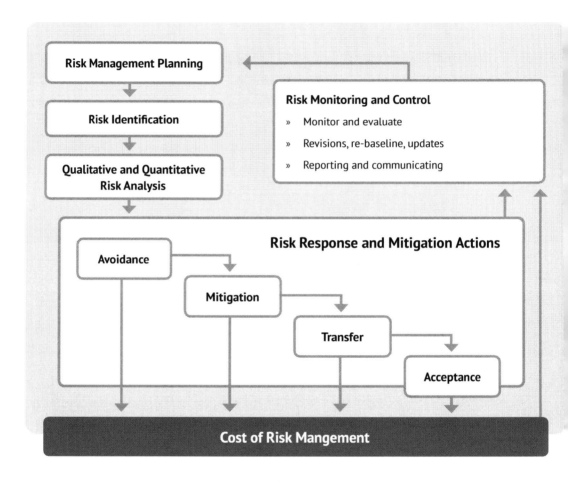

Owners and CMs must carefully review their respective risk management capabilities, which helps both parties understand the risk management roles for which they are best suited. The CM contract scope must clearly articulate these roles. As is also the case with safety, the CM should understand all the legal implications and responsibilities of providing risk management services. If neither party possesses the required skill set, the project team should retain an outside risk management consultant with construction expertise.

It is unreasonable to think that a construction project can eliminate all risks, but projects with risk management processes more easily identify risk events and manage them more efficiently than those without. The challenge is to recognize risk, decide what to do, and manage it. Construction management should integrate a risk management process to enhance project delivery and performance. The benefits of a risk management process include that it:

» Provides a disciplined framework to systematically guide risk identification and management that may not otherwise be considered.

» Helps avoid/reduce large losses and lessens the frequency of smaller losses.

» Helps identify opportunities that become realities and enhance the project delivery.

» Improves decision-making through clarifying responsibilities and authorities.

» Supports a better understanding for managing risks, leading to increased project confidence and improved allocation of resources.

Notes

Notes

CHAPTER 11

Program Management

11.1 Introduction

This section discusses program management, which in the construction industry context is the application of construction management to large, complex, or multiple capital improvement projects. A program manager (PgM) generally has the responsibility to manage all resources and relationships necessary to achieve an owner's desired outcome. Depending on the owner's organization and needs, in-house personnel or a contracted qualified consultant may provide program management services.

There are many similarities between project management and program management. Both utilize integrated systems and procedures such as budgeting, estimating, scheduling, procurement, and inspection to manage the design and construction process.

The principal differences between project management and program management are the number, size, complexity, and scope of the projects. Project management typically applies to a single project with sequential phasing. Program management often involves multiple projects occurring concurrently or at varying times. (See **Chapter 2: Project Management**.)

Generally, a program manager manages and coordinates a large capital program, potentially with multiple facilities in different locations. The program manager may manage or contract for activities that require owner involvement as well as the integration and coordination of any additional outsourced services that the owner's organization engaged.

Owners with significant in-house expertise may not contract for the full scope of a PgM's services but selectively choose services to supplement their own resources and expertise. The owner's needs and resources determine the scope of any contracted PgM's services. Regardless of who provides program management services, the PgM's roles and responsibilities remain the same.

Owners lacking the internal resources or expertise to perform program management may contract for full program management services in an "agency" (most common) or "at-risk" (less common) arrangement.

In an agency arrangement, the owner pays the PgM a fee to perform the owner's required services, which includes managing the other contracts directly between the owner and other professionals such as architects, engineers, CMs, and builders. An agency PgM advocates for the owner, but the PgM is not personally responsible for the other consultants' and contractors' performance. As such, the PgM is not liable for problems other team members create and does not have a duty to the other team members unless stated in the PgM's contract with the owner.

In an at-risk arrangement, the PgM is personally responsible for delivering the program's project elements according to the contract's requirements. The PgM may perform necessary services directly or hire sub-consultants and sub-contractors to assist. The PgM is ultimately responsible to the owner for the quality, cost, and schedule of all the deliverables within the contract's scope.

The owner and PgM may have conflicting interests because of an at-risk arrangement. The owner and PgM should always structure their contract to avoid or limit conflicts of interest and to avoid creating an adversarial relationship. When using the at-risk delivery method, the owner may want to hire a separate agency program management consultant to represent their interests.

An at-risk arrangement is better suited to construction management than the typical full portfolio of tasks under a program management contract. Program management activities are often more qualitative than quantitative and more often controlled by third parties, so the main disadvantage of at-risk is the difficulty in accurately defining the scope at the start. Construction contracting activities are generally better suited to well-defined cost and schedule control measures. Where parts of scope definition and risk allocation are not well-defined, a CMAR contract is preferable to an at-risk PgM contract.

11.2   Pre-Design Phase

In the beginning, many owners consider what organizational capabilities they need and decide that their ability to execute a major program is limited by a lack of staff and sometimes the necessary expertise to define and manage the program on a sustained basis.

Therefore, the owner acquires the necessary expertise by contracting with an independent entity (such as a firm or firms) that can provide the necessary staff and expertise to support the program.

There are various approaches when outsourcing program management services. Some owners prefer to retain most of the program control and will integrate an outside firm's staff into their own organization. Other owners will engage a program management firm to fully staff and manage their program.

When the PgM starts early in the program development phase, it is the greatest opportunity to improve a program's chances for success. This involvement may include actively defining objectives and concepts as well as the acceptance and operation of the completed projects on behalf of the owner. The PgM ideally makes initial strategic, technical, and business decisions that become the basis for the capital improvement program. As the program is defined, a full program management plan (PgMP) develops that then becomes the program's governance document.

Additionally, the PgM needs to identify and address regulatory requirements. These may include the environmental, local permitting, and other necessary regulatory requirements that could hurt the program's successful delivery if not addressed early in the process.

THE PROGRAM MANAGEMENT TEAM

In this early stage, the core program management team is usually small. The team may include the program manager, planners, schedulers, conceptual estimators, financial experts, lawyers, and other needed front-end experts. These professionals may be from within the owner's organization, the selected PgM firm, or the various specialty firms in the program management team. The program may introduce personnel on an as-needed consulting basis to meet specific needs. Part-time professionals who supplement the core team help the core team stay small and efficient.

The program management contract should clearly convey the roles and authority the owner gives to the program management team. A best practice is to create a responsibility matrix that defines the specific deliverables and each party's role to provide those deliverables. The PgM and owner should draft and agree on an organization chart with task descriptions. It should also include a decision matrix that shows how to formulate specific recommendations and who makes final decisions.

Program management works best when the PgM:

» Has a clearly defined scope of work.

» Has clearly defined responsibilities.

» Is an integral part (or extension) of the owner's staff.

The project controls team should form during this early phase as an essential part of the program management team. Proper budget, schedule, and document control help determine a project's success just as much as the technical success of the constructed facilities. This group's key personnel may include cost control engineers, schedulers, estimators, programmers, and administrators who assist the PgM in developing the program's overall scope, cost, and schedule.

The project controls system is the backbone of the program. Early establishment of good project controls will enable managers to identify, assess, and manage program trends quickly and effectively.

PROGRAM MANAGEMENT PLAN (PGMP)

The owner approves the written PgMP, which is the master reference document for the program management team, and provides guidance to the entire project team from inception through planning, design, construction, and closeout. It is a living document that the team must update periodically throughout the program's life. The PgMP defines the program's following elements:

» Vision	» Policies
» Implementation strategy	» Procedures
» Schedule	» Standards
» Budget criteria	

The PgMP provides a level of continuity and standardization across the program to facilitate effective communications and decision-making. It serves as an organization's formal process for reviewing, evaluating, prioritizing, documenting, approving, implementing, and maintaining all its projects within the program.

The components of a PgMP are similar to those of the PMP, but unlike a PMP, the PgMP addresses common elements across the entire program rather than one specific project. A project management plan may or may not be needed for specific projects within a program, depending on the level of detail contained in the program management plan. (See **Chapter 2: Project Management**.)

PROGRAM MANAGEMENT OFFICE (PGMO)

Certain agencies and owner organizations establish a formal Program Management Office (PgMO) to oversee and implement all projects within the program. The PgMO is a management team concept and process that is seamlessly integrated and planned collaboratively. Within the PgMO, governance responsibilities and task ownership must be clear. A PgMO that follows best practices will have a strong charter that defines program success, typically in terms of quality work, safe work, the scope of work, work on schedule, and work within budget.

The PgMO organization or team must be well-coordinated, fully integrated, and high performing. The team should have the responsibility to oversee program delivery within six key functional areas:

1. Understand the owner's needs and translate them into a capital program.
2. Set project delivery strategy, define the project functions, and select delivery teams.
3. Control program execution through budgets and schedules, procedures, documentation, and communication.
4. Provide status reporting.
5. Effectively close out the program.
6. Collect and institutionalize best practices and lessons learned.

Organizations that follow best practices invest in project management skills training for staff to achieve project delivery consistency and to reduce project failures. These organizations also have an executive group that has the overall management responsibility to monitor performance measurement systems.

PgMO organizations implement a review process that uses real-time metrics to track program performance, such as scope, budget, and schedule. As a best practice, these organizations link and align their performance measurement systems (scorecards) with long-range goals and strategic objectives. They also value and measure individual input in the form of satisfaction surveys to key stakeholders (e.g., user groups, consultants, and contractors). These organizations continuously improve their program management methodologies.

MANAGEMENT INFORMATION SYSTEM (MIS)

Large capital improvement programs generate a tremendous amount of data, which must be organized, analyzed, and easily accessed and reported. The program team must communicate this data and other information at all levels within the team. The PgM should constantly communicate about issues related to design, costs, schedule, and other program concerns. The PgM must establish an environment that facilitates and encourages designers, sub-consultants, and affected parties to communicate regularly and effectively.

Web-based project management systems are the standard tool to manage information for large programs. Web-based systems allow large and geographically dispersed teams to communicate constantly and to document this communication. System characteristics vary but generally include the following:

» Document control

» Budget tracking

» Cost tracking

» Commitment tracking

» Communication tools

» A calendar

» Review and approval functions

The PgM should formulate specific criteria for the MIS to control and report the program's progress. An owner may or may not already have adequate or appropriate systems for a major program's additional data and documentation. The MIS must report progress, schedule, costs, scope changes, and quality compliance in a standard electronic format available to every entity engaged in the program. The PgM must determine the best level of data sharing and system integration.

The PgM must also establish the flow of documentation and make an early decision to capture, archive, and distribute documents in either an electronic or hard copy mode. Electronic document control for large capital improvement programs can be cost-effective and provides many side benefits that are essential to large capital programs. (See **Chapter 9: Technology Management**.)

SCOPE DEFINITION

The program team must establish detailed procedures to control the program's administration, accounting, and management when they establish the MIS. The priority at the earliest stage is to validate the need for the program and determine its fiscal viability. The PgM must provide reasonable cost estimates based on realistic schedules, the full scope of work, and the agreed level of quality.

At this stage, the PgM must anticipate potential delays and other risk factors to establish appropriate program contingencies. A risk register should track these potential impacts. (See **Chapter 10: Risk Management**.)

The PgM must identify the scope of as many related requirements as possible. These may include environmental studies, sustainability, wetland preservation, archaeological investigations, historic preservation, and entitlement considerations, among other activities leading to the final permits. Each will have an impact on the program's scope, cost, and schedule.

Once the program quantities are known and the owner agrees, the next step is to develop the program's quality, schedule, scope, and cost.

The level of quality is one of the most difficult areas to define and communicate in writing. All parties must understand that the level of quality affects all areas, but most importantly the final cost of the improvements. Quality may also dramatically impact the length of time required to design and construct the program. The PgM, with the support of planners and designers, must establish the quality standards each consultant and contractor will meet. This may result in a set of simple program quality guidelines or a detailed quality standards manual.

The owner approves the final scope of work. It is based on detailed working sessions with the owner as well as other stakeholders. The owner approves an established realistic budget and schedule that include cost escalations, market conditions, risk assessment, and appropriate design and construction contingencies.

The owner may request a study of various strategies to improve program cost or schedule, including using various delivery methods in one program. The PgM may also examine a strategy to divide the program into manageable segments or projects. This process may go through numerous cycles before finding the ideal solution.

Once the owner approves the execution strategy, the PgM fully documents and includes it in the PgMP along with the resulting budget, overall scope of work, quality standards, program schedule, and the major critical milestones for the program's successful implementation.

PROGRAM EVALUATION

Throughout the program, the PgM holds "lessons learned" sessions to continuously improve the program. These lessons learned sessions should identify program strengths and weaknesses as well as how to improve performance. The program evaluation typically covers the entire architectural, engineering, procurement, and construction performance, as well as the post-construction phase.

11.3   Design Phase

The PgM manages a program of multiple projects or a large project with multiple elements. Therefore, each of these projects or project elements uses and repeats project management techniques. At the program level, the PgM focuses on each project's design aspects in the program and how they relate based on program design standards established at the program's beginning.

The PgM establishes clear design direction across the program and integrates all the program elements and individual projects to include changes that may evolve.

DESIGN ORGANIZATION STRUCTURE

The PgM establishes the organizational structure so that the required resources are available to complete designs for individual projects within the required schedule, budget, and quality standards. This structure should also help the program elements integrate and the program management team communicate within the team. The design organization structure may include several design teams as well as consider client/owner policies such as the inclusion of disadvantaged, local, and small businesses. The structure must be flexible enough to provide a balanced pool of resources during periods of uneven workload.

The PgM assists the owner and leads in the design team(s) selection. The PgM establishes a scope of services for each project and standardizes the selection process. The PgM helps the owner develop a "standard" contract form for the scope of services or uses industry-standard contract forms. The PgM must also help the owner establish program guidelines for design and consultant fees.

DESIGN CRITERIA

The PgM oversees the development of the design standards and criteria, a crucial step to successfully implement a large program. Clear and executable design criteria promote design consistency and maximize design efficiency. Such efforts will assure consistency among all projects in the program and assist in controlling construction costs, expediting procurement, and improving ease of maintenance.

The design standards and criteria should address space and functionality, codes and standards, O&M, safety and security, and local market conditions (such as availability of materials). All appropriate project team members should receive the design standards so that they understand the expected level of quality.

At this stage, the PgM's priority is to deliver a design that meets the owner's criteria and apply a realistic construction methodology consistently across the overall design program. This usually includes identifying the code requirements and refining the finished product's quality standards.

DESIGN DEVELOPMENT

Project design development in large programs may be simultaneous, in overlapping sequence, or in series.

The PgM must focus on the overall design program so that the various designers adhere to schedule and deliver coordinated work products. The PgM must establish a comprehensive design review process and advise the owner of any deviation from approved program performance standards. The PgM monitors design contract costs as well as construction budget estimates for consistency with overall program budgets. The PgM must promote designs with an eye toward consistency, initial capital costs, and lifecycle costing that includes O&M.

The PgM should constantly try to improve the individual designs using lessons learned from earlier projects, construction RFI, bids, and shared experience within the program. The PgM may work with the owner to establish criteria for all phases of the program to optimize the flow of information among all the program participants.

The PgM must also seek opportunities for cost and time savings through VE and applicable peer reviews. The PgM facilitates constructability reviews for project designs, reviews projected construction costs that the designers and contractors provide, and then prepares independent check estimates so that the project stays within budget. The project may use an independent cost estimator to check cost estimates.

BIM brings the previously separate functions of planning, design, construction, commissioning, and maintenance/management together as an integrated whole. Lifecycle cost factors then use BIM, constructability review, and other tools to further reduce costs.

CONSTRUCTION CONTRACT PACKAGING

The PgM often helps the owner shape the overall design program into executable contract packages that meet the owner's scheduling and operational needs. In this effort, the PgM focuses on the integration of the overall design program and the various design packages' scope, design, phasing, and schedule to comply with the owner's goals.

The PgM either uses industry-standard contracts or helps the owner develop a customized construction contract that meets the program's needs. Depending on those needs, the PgM may also recommend and assist with alternative project delivery methods. In some cases, multiple project delivery methods within a program may be better.

OWNER-PURCHASED MATERIALS AND EQUIPMENT

The PgM investigates the potential benefits of the owner purchasing materials and equipment for the program in bulk and provides recommendations to the owner. After the owner agrees, the PgM and the designers develop appropriate contract documents for procurement. The PgM monitors the procurement of owner-furnished materials and equipment to ensure that the projects' schedule and construction coordination needs are met.

QUALITY MANAGEMENT

The design review process must have consistency across the entire program. The designer must clearly understand the standards and expectations for evaluating the design, and this must be consistent from beginning to end. As much as possible, the same review team should participate at each stage of the design process. This provides consistency and efficiency, resulting in better value to the owner and better project quality.

The PgM reviews designs to verify the 5 C's:

1. Clarity

2. Completeness

3. Compliance with program and design criteria

4. Coordination across disciplines

5. Constructability

The PgM monitors the design team's compliance with the program's QMP and document control plan. Steps to enhance design quality may include peer reviews of designs and periodic audits of the design manager's records.

COST MANAGEMENT

The PgM's responsibilities for cost management during design include the management and monitoring of design costs, estimating costs of facilities under design, and overall program costs. Program cost management during design involves a disciplined approach to establish and manage the allocation of project and program contingencies. The PgM maintains up-to-date local market construction cost information and pricing indices to ensure the accuracy of construction cost estimates and budgets.

The PgM also manages program costs using construction contract packaging. The PgM adds value by monitoring market conditions, conducting contractor outreach workshops, adjusting contract packaging, and revising the timing of bid advertisements to attract more competition. The PgM should consider that large programs often have big impacts on local construction markets.

The PgM's cost management may include generating and managing the program's cash flow projections. This is especially critical on programs with revenue from bond sales, tax levies, or other financing mechanisms.

Program cost management is very different from a single project's cost management. On a single project, cost control traditionally includes making estimates, establishing a budget, revising estimates as design progresses, diligently preventing scope creep, and staying on budget at the end. **If the PgM views a program this way (as a series of independent projects, each with its own contingency), then the program will likely exceed the original budget.**

Over a program's life, there are more opportunities than in a single project for owners to change their requirements as well as more pricing variability and uncertainty. Budget management in a program must account for the entire program to manage and balance changes more effectively. This often requires using a program-level contingency and adjusting the overall scope and budget to balance objectives with the budget.

TIME MANAGEMENT

The PgM must continue to develop and update the program master schedule. On a large program, the master schedule should include all interdependencies between projects. As individual projects start in the program, additional detailed schedules must develop based on the overall milestones set at the program level.

Before the end of the design phase, the PgM recommends incorporating the project schedule and other time-related specifications that are appropriate for the specific project and the overall program. From a program perspective, it is important that the PgM identifies the interfacing milestones and provides the appropriate coordination language to address schedule overlap and mitigate schedule impacts because of delays to project interfaces.

Clear, concise, unambiguous scheduling specifications are critical and cannot be overemphasized.

11.4   Procurement Phase

PROCUREMENT SCOPE

The procurement function can last from inception until final acceptance by the owner/operator. It can include multiple phases and functions, such as:

» Upfront professional services to develop a business plan or implementation plan.
» A/E design services to develop a concept and detailed design documents.
» CM services to provide constructability reviews, project estimates, and to manage the construction phase.
» CMAR or general contractor services to build the facility.
» Start-up and commissioning services that can work with the owner/operator to accept and operate the facility.

Typically, procurement includes advertising, the request for proposals or bids, pre-proposal/pre-bid meetings, addenda, receipt of proposals/bids, bid review and recommendation, and contract award.

Additionally, procurement occurs at different times throughout programs with multiple projects. It is important to identify standard procurement documents and strategies early in the program.

The PgM's procurement responsibility can start before there is a definition of scope and services to procure. PgMs can advise owners as to funding, permitting, contract packaging, phasing, interdependencies, design standards, and the management organization as well as contract strategy and contract methodology.

PROCUREMENT STRATEGY

The PgMP should include a procurement strategy based on identified projects, the scope of work documentation, order of magnitude budgets, and program phasing. The owner may already have procurement procedures or the program management organization may need to develop and implement procedures.

The PgM recommends a strategy for how to package (number of contracts) and deliver (e.g., design-build, traditional/design-bid-build, CMAR, etc.) the various program elements.

Many PgMs miss or spend too little time deciding what contract packages and type of delivery are the most time and cost-effective for the owner. It is an important step because the number of contracts and the delivery method not only affect owner risk but also drive how much planning, design, construction contract, and management costs are necessary to implement the program.

PGM ROLE IN PROCUREMENT

The owner can use its organization, a PgM, or a combination of resources to provide procurement services.

As the scope of services is defined, the PgM recommends what scope and services need further clarification through planning, what can move to conceptual and detailed design, as well as what construction to manage and how. The PgM helps the owner develop scope and procurement documentation for proposal or bidding purposes that include estimates, design standards, and schedules.

The PgM must advise the owner on the sequence of the projects in the program. Availability of funding, program priorities, interdependencies among projects, contract packaging, and phasing are all factors that affect overall decision-making and scheduling.

Procurement strategies also have budget implications. When formulating the preliminary project budget, the procurement strategies to discuss and agree upon include:

» Pre-design and pre-construction support services.
» Design-Bid-Build, CMAR, or design-build project delivery methods.
» Contract pricing strategies (firm fixed price or lump sum contracts, cost-reimbursement contracts, unit price contracts, etc.).
» Owner furnished equipment or materials and long lead items.
» Property acquisition strategy.

» Utility relocation strategy.

» O&M strategy (including operation by the Program Manager).

Any or all of these are issues to consider when developing potential procurement strategies, depending on the program's nature as well as the legal and financial constraints. They will all have budget impacts that the PgM must consider to reach the initial construction and program budgets.

MARKET ANALYSIS/BID OPPORTUNITY COMMUNICATIONS

The PgM can provide a detailed market analysis of the potential construction bidding climate. The PgM can determine the global availability of labor, equipment, and material resources as well as tailor this information to meet specific owner requirements, such as minority business enterprise (MBE) participation.

In some cases, the PgM may conduct industry outreach to attract proposers/bidders. This could involve developing tailored presentations to the design and construction industry as well as the media to publicize the program and market the potential commercial opportunities. These initial orientation forums are good tools to inform the industry and help encourage more competition.

SCHEDULE AND DOCUMENT MANAGEMENT

In the procurement phase, the PgM recommends a program schedule and other time-related specifications that are appropriate for the specific project and the overall program, consistent with the size and complexity of the work. This provides a level of understanding and builds confidence with the owner and contractors. From a program perspective, the PgM identifies the interfacing milestones and provides the appropriate coordination language to address schedule overlap and to mitigate schedule impacts because of delays to project interfaces.

Clear, concise, unambiguous scheduling specifications are critical and cannot be overemphasized.

11.5   Construction Phase

During construction, the PgM oversees and monitors the construction activities on all the program's projects and elements. Since construction occurs over varying windows, the PgM must monitor for status, trends, potential impacts, and other items that could affect the total program.

The PgM's objective during construction is to expedite and enhance the efficiency of the construction process. The PgM plans, organizes, openly communicates, and facilitates the process with a focus on fulfilling the owner's scope, cost, quality, and time requirements for the entire program.

PROVISION OF ON-SITE FACILITIES

When part of the PgM's requested services, the PgM plans the logistical support needed to effectively manage construction. This can occur early in the planning process. Based on the scope, contract packaging assumptions, and the construction work's geographic location, the PgM develops plans for centralized or common office and site facilities for use by all entities engaged in the program. This space may be in the owner's facilities, the PgM's facilities, or in new site facilities.

Physical on-site co-location of all key project stakeholders is a best practice, but electronic meeting software allows for good collaboration without being physically present on-site.

COORDINATION AND COMMUNICATION

The PgM provides coordination and leadership on program communications. The PgM must understand the roles and responsibilities within the owner's organization and program team to determine what information needs to be communicated to whom and when. The PgM's challenge is to foster a work environment of open communication with the right procedures and documentation at the right level. The PgM must establish this balance with procedures and reporting requirements so that communications are organized and consistent across the program.

To monitor the program, the PgM continually measures the progress of each project, identifies the key interfacing milestones among projects and their impact on the program, and facilitates all stakeholder actions to accommodate individual project needs while avoiding impacts to the program. The goal is to maximize the program's efficiency from planning through construction to achieve program success on time, within budget, and at the expected level of quality.

PROGRAM PROGRESS MEETINGS

The PgM conducts periodic program progress meetings and provides periodic performance/status reports to the owner. The PgM conducts these meetings with representatives of the various projects. Where owner protocols do not exist, the PgM establishes the reporting criteria, format, and performance metrics such as a critical path schedule, cash flow curves, work placement rates, and budget/cost reports.

The PgM may monitor program performance by chairing or facilitating these project review meetings, which may cover safety, quality, schedule, cost, and operational issues. These meetings and the information presented provide the basis for decision-making and coordination among the various stakeholders. Typically, program meetings occur once a month, but smaller individual and project-specific meetings happen more frequently or as needed.

TIME MANAGEMENT

The PgM establishes procedures to plan and monitor compliance with the program timeline on the program master schedule. The PgM also establishes the program's overall phasing and contract packaging. After defining the logic, sequencing, and interfacing milestones, the PgM develops the program schedule, overall durations for the projects, and the program's critical path.

A critical dates list documents key milestone and interface dates. The various contract documents also incorporate these dates. During the construction phase, the PgM monitors the contractors' CPM schedule updates for compliance with all required critical dates. Throughout the program, project activities may be adjusted to maintain the most efficient and effective program schedule with an optimal balance of time, cost, safety, and quality goals.

BUDGET AND COST MONITORING

The PgM constantly reviews and monitors program budgets, commitments, and costs to make sure the overall program tracks as planned. The program may require budget revisions throughout to adjust funding from one project to another or from one cost element to another.

As scopes and costs become more definitive, updates to the program budget reflect the latest cost to budget comparisons. The objective is to manage the incurred costs, estimated costs, and costs to complete to stay within the program budget. With actual cost trend measurements, the PgM recommends additional options to manage the overall program budget.

FUNDING/CASH FLOW

The PgM forecasts cash flows throughout the life of the program, first based on the initial budget assessments then later with actual defined costs and forecasts. Using time and cost management techniques, the PgM informs the owner of cash needs to develop the program financial plan, in particular the timing of available funding sources.

CHANGE ORDERS

The PgM helps the owner establish the change order management procedures and reports as well as monitors the program's change order process across all contracts. Whether the change is to a design contract or construction contract, the process must document and implement the authorization, notice, and direction to the designer/contractor in an efficient and cost-effective manner. The PgM must provide accurate facts and sound advice to the owner to handle change decisions quickly and effectively.

CLAIMS MANAGEMENT

The PgM monitors the claims management process throughout the program. Resolving claims on one project may set a precedent for other projects within the program, so the PgM must recommend ways to minimize the overall impact on the program. The program procedures and construction contract documents should address claims management, including:

» Merit evaluations

» Entitlement evaluation

» Negotiations

» Settlement procedures

» Handling of disputes

» Appeal procedures

QUALITY MANAGEMENT

The PgM and the owner establish the program's quality standards and, along with the CM, the procedures for meeting contract requirements. Quality procedures typically define QC and QA responsibilities. The PgM monitors and provides oversight during the design process and works with the project team to ensure quality during the construction process.

The PgM is also responsible for quality management in the administration of the program itself. In addition to assuring the quality of each project within the program, the PgM implements policies and procedures for the whole program and evaluates if they meet quality standards for effective implementation, continuity, and recordkeeping.

The PgM must ensure that all projects are managed to achieve the quality standards set for the program. The design and construction documents must clearly define QC and QA responsibilities. The PgM and each project's CM monitor the performance of the team's inspection and testing for QC and QA so that all projects have consistent inspections that meet the program's established quality standards.

DOCUMENT CONTROL

The PgM and the owner establish procedures for document control, recordkeeping, and file retention. The PgM also defines document control procedures for continuity and consistency among all projects. The PgM may also establish and implement the management system necessary to receive, record, track, distribute, and file all documentation from program initiation documents to final project record drawings.

The PgM and owner establish procedures to identify, distribute, handle, and store records early in the program. The ability to effectively manage documentation flow is critical to program communications and decision-making.

MANAGEMENT REPORTING

The PgM monitors the reporting system that was established early in the program and generates a monthly status report for the owner. This program report summarizes the status and issues regarding scope, cost, quality, safety, and schedule for all the projects in the program.

11.6   Post-Construction Phase

PROGRAM COMPLETION

Program completion requires procedures to close out all program contractual and administrative activities. After substantial completion of a program segment or individual project, the PgM monitors the closeout of each project and verifies completion through the individual CM for that project. Closeout items include completion of:

» All construction contract punchlists and issuance of substantial completion.

» Settlement of all changes and claims.

» Submittal to the owner of required documents such as warranties, O&M manuals, and record drawings.

» Acceptable disposition of spare parts.

» Confirmation that O&M and training are complete.

» Confirmation that grant or funding provisions are satisfied.

» Receipt of signed releases from the contractors and issuance of final payment.

» Demobilization of contractor facilities.

PROGRAM PROJECTS INTERFACE

The PgM coordinates the completion and turnover of individual projects and monitors the remaining interfaces with other projects still under construction in the program. These interfaces with active projects are often critical.

When facilities/temporary infrastructure are needed before other projects are complete, the PgM must identify the temporary infrastructure scope and cost and incorporate the work into the program to allow full activation of the facilities being turned over. Phasing of projects is another program management function that promotes the efficient use of completed projects or parts of projects to maximize the owner's ROI.

OPERATION AND MAINTENANCE MANAGEMENT

O&M management support is an extension of the startup or activation process and should include adequate staffing and resources. It is based on advanced planning that should happen when the planning process begins and may include staff training.

The PgM helps the owner with a new program's maintenance management. The PgM's responsibilities may include maintenance efforts, schedule, materials required, and spare parts inventory. Typically, the PgM ensures that the O&M manuals, as-built drawings, and spare parts lists comply with the owner's current O&M management system.

TURNOVER (ACTIVATION OR STARTUP)

Program turnover (or activation) is the process of transitioning from construction to permanent operation of a facility. During this phase, the owner or owner's staff prepare to accept and operate a new facility or facilities.

To help manage the turnover functions, the PgM helps the owner define staff planning, service contract requirements, and facility requirements that are not provided in the construction contract, operational planning, and operational assessments. The goal is to obtain maximum utilization of the facility at the least cost in parallel with the design and construction process and to integrate the facility into the production and operations plans and schedules.

On major programs, the turnover process may include a sequential startup process to bring various facilities or components online and test those facilities or components under real conditions before acceptance for permanent operations. Turnover should have high visibility throughout program development and execution. Third-party commissioning agents frequently lead the system startup efforts throughout a project.

The PgM may help the owner develop staff plans based on the transition of ownership and a schedule to mobilize the owner's staff. The PgM may also help the owner develop and administer procedures for warranty administration to assure that defective work is resolved in a timely manner.

FACILITY MANAGEMENT

In large and complex programs, the operation, maintenance, and funding commitments are often key to meeting the program objectives. For example, build, operate, and transfer (BOT) programs often have a significant operational period with specific maintenance and repair obligations as well as expansion milestones based on agreed demand.

The owner may retain the PgM through the operational period to oversee and monitor program objectives. The PgM has intimate knowledge of the program and a long-term relationship with the owner, so the PgM is normally well-suited to this facility management role.

ADMINISTRATIVE CLOSEOUT

The PgM's administrative closeout responsibilities involve demobilizing the program team, completing activities with other stakeholders, arranging the disposition of program records, closing of funding/financing agreements, and performing an evaluation of program success and lessons learned. The PgM follows the procedures specified in each contract's terms and conditions to settle and close the project's design and construction contracts. The PgM helps the owner's finance staff close out funding to the program or projects. The PgM reviews the PMP to verify that all program elements are complete.

Notes

Notes

Appendix I: Table of Abbreviations

ADM – Arrow Diagramming Method

AIA – American Institute of Architects

ANSI – American National Standards Institute

AR – Augmented Reality

BIM – Building Information Modeling

BOCA – Building Officials and Code Administrators

BOT – Build, operate, and transfer

BREEAM – Building Research Environment Assessment Method

CHST – Construction Health and Safety Technician

CIEB – Continual Improvement of Existing Buildings

CIH – Certified Industrial Hygienist

CCM - Certified Construction Manager

CM – Construction manager

CMAR – Construction manager at-risk

CMMC – Cybersecurity Maturity Model Certification

CMP – Construction management plan

CO – Certificate of Occupancy

CPM – Critical Path Method

CSI – Construction Specifications Institute

CSP – Certified Safety Professional

CVS – Certified Value Specialist

DBIA – Design-Build Institute of America

DER – Distributed Energy Resource

DRB – Disputes Review Board

EPA – Environmental Protection Agency

EPC – Engineering, Procurement, Construction

EPCM – Engineering, Procurement, Construction Management

EVA – Earned Value Analysis

EVM – Earned Value Management

FedRAMP – Federal Risk and Authorization Management Program

FISMA – Federal Information Security Management Act

GBCA – Green Building Council of Australia

GBI – Green Building Initiative

GMP - Guaranteed Maximum Price

ICE - Independent Cost Estimate

IDIQ – Indefinite Delivery / Indefinite Quantity

IPD – Integrated Project Delivery

JHA – Job hazard analysis

JOC – Job Order Contracting

LEED – Leadership in Energy and Environmental Design

MATOC – Multiple Award Task Order Contract

MBE – Minority business enterprise

MIS – Management Information System

NC – New Construction

NFPA – National Fire Protection Association

NMS – National Master Specification

NTP – Notice to Proceed

O&M – Operation and Maintenance

OCIP – Owner Controlled Insurance Program

OPR – Owner's Project Requirements

OSHA – Occupational Safety and Health Administration

PCP – Project Commissioning Plan

PDM – Precedence Diagramming Method

PgM – Program manager

PgMO – Program management office

PgMP – Program management plan

PM – Project manager

PMP – Project management plan

PPM – Project Procedures Manual

QA – Quality assurance

QC – Quality control

QM – Quality Management

QMP – Quality Management Plan

QMS – Quality Management System

RFI – Requests for Information

RFP – Requests for Proposals

RFQ – Request for Qualifications

RIR – Recordable Incident Rates

ROI – Return on Investment

SATOC – Single Award Task Order Contract

SOQ – Statements of Qualifications

UFGS – Unified Facilities Guide Specifications

USGBC – U.S. Green Building Council

VE – Value engineering

VDC – Virtual Design and Construction

VR – Virtual Reality

Appendix II: Definitions

The terms contained in these definitions are intended to convey a specific meaning as utilized in these standards. All other technical terminology herein may be presumed to follow accepted industry usage.

A

Addendum
A supplement to documents, issued prior to taking receipt of bids, for the purpose of clarifying, correcting, or otherwise changing bid documents previously issued.

Additional Services
Services provided in addition to those specifically designated as basic services in the agreement between the owner and CM. Also known as supplemental services.

Agency
A legal relationship by which one party (agent) is empowered and obligated to act on behalf of another party (owner).

Agency Construction Management
A form of construction management performed in a defined relationship between the CM and owner. The agency form of construction management establishes a specific role of the CM acting as the owner's principal agent in connection with the project/program.

Agreement
A document setting forth the relationships and obligations between two parties, as the CM and owner or contractor and owner. It may incorporate other documents by reference.

Apparent Low Bidder
The bidder who has submitted the lowest bid for a division of work described in bid documents, a proposal form, or proposed contract.

Approved Bidders List
The list of contractors that have been prequalified for the purpose of submitting responsible, competitive bids.

Approved Changes

Changes in the contract documents that have been subjected to an agreed upon change approval process and have been approved by the party empowered to approve such changes. See "Change Order."

Artificial Intelligence (AI)

A technology that applies computer algorithms to replicate actions that humans perform.

As-Built Drawings

Drawings (plans) that show the work as actually installed.

At-Risk Construction Management

A delivery method that entails a commitment by the construction manager to deliver the project for an established amount, often a guaranteed maximum price (GMP). The construction manager acts as a consultant to the owner in the development and design phases. During construction, the CM will assume additional obligations and will undertake construction responsibilities, typically being placed in a legal position like that of a general contractor.

Augmented Reality (AR)

An interactive tool that overlays digital information onto real-world objects.

B

Basic Services

Scope of service as defined in the original agreement between the owner and CM as basic services.

Beneficial Occupancy

The use of the constructed facility by the owner prior to final completion of the construction.

Bid

An offer to perform the work described in contract documents at a specified cost.

Biddability

The degree to which a set of bid documents could be reasonably expected to permit a bidder to establish a competitive price to perform the work as defined in the bid documents.

Biddability Review

A formal review of the contract documents, addendum, and reference documents to be accomplished with respect to the local construction marketplace and the bid packaging strategy to eliminate ambiguities, errors, omissions, and contradictions, for the purpose of minimizing bid prices in the procurement phase and disputes during construction.

Bid Documents

The documents issued to the contractor(s) by the owner that describe the proposed work and contract terms. Bid documents typically include drawings, specifications, contract forms, general and supplementary general conditions, proposal, or bid forms, and other information.

Bid Bond

A pledge from a surety to pay up to the bond amount to the owner in the event the bidder defaults on its commitment to enter into a contract to perform the work described in the bid documents for the bid price. The bond is designed to protect the owner for the difference in price between the accepted bid and the next lowest acceptable bid.

Bond

A pledge from a surety guaranteeing the performance of the obligation defined in the bond, including the completion of work or payment of the bond amount to the obligee (owner or contractor) in the event of a default, or non-payment by a principal (contractor or subcontractor), as with bid, performance and labor and material bonds.

Bonus

Additional compensation paid or to be paid to the contractor by the owner as a reward for accomplishing predetermined objectives that are over and above the basic requirements of the contract between the owner and contractor.

Budget

The dollar amount and planned allocation of resources by the owner for a project/program.

Budget Estimate

An estimate of the cost of work based on preliminary information, with a qualified degree of accuracy.

Building Commissioning (Cx)

A systematic process of ensuring that all building systems perform interactively according to the design intent and the owner's operational needs. The process evaluates building equipment, subsystems, operation and maintenance (O&M) procedures, and performance of all building components to ensure that they function efficiently, and as designed, as a system.

Building Information Modeling (BIM)

A method to create a digital representation of the physical and functional characteristics of a facility that a project team can virtually analyze, document, and assess, then revise iteratively throughout the design and construction process.

Building Research Environment Assessment Method (BREEAM)

A UK standard environmental assessment method and rating system for buildings that has established best practices for sustainable building design, construction, and operation and has become one of the most comprehensive and widely recognized measures of a building's environmental performance. It encourages designers, clients, and others to think about low carbon and low impact design, minimizing the energy demands created by a building before considering energy efficiency, and low carbon technologies.

Business Intelligence (BI)

The process of transforming raw data into actionable data.

C

Changed Conditions

Conditions or circumstances, physical or otherwise, which differ from the conditions or circumstances on which the contract documents were based.

Change Order

A written agreement or directive between contracted parties, which represents an addition, deletion, or revision to the contract documents, identifies the change in price and time and describes the nature (scope) of the work involved. A document directing a change in scope.

Claim

A formal demand requesting additional time, money, or both for acts or omissions during the performance of the work filed by a contractor or the owner with the other party, in accordance with the provisions of the contract documents.

Clash Detection

Within the context of BIM, a method to check for interferences by searching for intersecting volumes.

Code of Accounts

A systematic numeric accounting method of identifying various categories of costs incurred in the progress of a project. The segregation of engineering, procurement, fabrication, construction, and associated project costs into elements for accounting purposes.

Commissioning (Cx)

A process that includes the startup, calibration, and certification of a facility. ASHRAE defines commissioning as "a quality-oriented process for achieving, verifying, and documenting that the performance of facilities, systems, and assemblies meets defined objectives and criteria."

Construction Technology

The systems, tools, equipment, and software used to organize and manipulate data, materials, and other resources to complete a capital construction project.

CM Fee

A form of contractual payment for services, where the CM is paid a fee for services performed.

Contingency

An amount of money reserved by the owner to pay for unforeseen changes in the work or increases in cost.

Constructability

The ease with which a project can be built, based upon the clarity, consistency, and completeness of the contract documents for bidding, administration, and interpretation to achieve overall project objectives.

Constructability Review

The process of evaluating the construction documents for clarity, consistency, completeness, and ease of construction to facilitate the achievement of overall project objectives.

Construction Budget

The sum established, normally during the pre-design or design phase, as available for construction of the project.

Construction Costs

The cost of all work required to complete the construction as defined in the construction contract documents.

Construction Management

A professional management practice applied to construction projects from project inception to completion for the purpose of controlling time, cost, scope, and quality.

Construction Management Plan (CMP)

The CMP is a written, project-specific plan that outlines the project's scope, budget, schedule, organizational roles, quality standards, and specific methods and procedures that the CM will undertake to accomplish the various management tasks for the project.

Construction Manager (CM)

An organization or individual with the expertise and resources to provide construction management services.

Construction Schedule

A graphic, tabular, or narrative representation or depiction of the time of construction of the project, showing activities and duration of activities in sequential order.

Contract Administration

The function of implementing the terms and conditions of a contract, based upon established systems, policies, and procedures.

Contractor

The organization or individual who undertakes responsibility for the performance of the work, in accordance with plans, specifications and contract documents, providing and controlling the labor, material and equipment to accomplish the work.

Construction Contract Documents

The documents which provide the basis for the contract entered into between parties. They typically include the bid documents updated to reflect the agreement between the owner and the contractor(s).

Cost Control

The function of limiting the cost of the construction project to the established budget based upon owner-approved procedures and authority.

Cost Management

The act of managing all or partial costs of a planning, design, and construction process to remain within the owner's budget.

Cost of Construction

All costs attributed to the construction of the project, including the cost of contracts with the contractor(s), construction support items, general condition items, all purchased labor, material, and fixed equipment.

Critical Path Method (CPM)

A scheduling technique used to plan and control a project. CPM combines all relevant information into a single plan defining the sequence and duration of operations and depicting the interrelationship of the work elements required to complete the project. The critical path is defined as the longest sequence of activities in a network that establishes the minimum length of time for accomplishment of the end event of the project. Arrow Diagramming Method (ADM) and Precedence Diagramming Method (PDM) are both common forms of CPM scheduling.

Cybersecurity

A practice to allow project stakeholders to access appropriate information from digital systems and devices while also protecting that data from unauthorized persons/entities.

D

Descope Meeting

A meeting with the apparent low bidder to analyze and discuss the important elements of the project, such as schedule, detailed project requirements, unusual elements of construction, and sustainability goals, to ensure the bidder's submission is accurate.

Design-Build

A project delivery method, which combines architectural and engineering design, services with construction performance under one contract agreement.

Designer

The individual or organization that performs the design and prepares plans and specifications for the work to be performed. The designer can be an architect, an engineer, or an organization, which combines design services with other professional services.

Design – Final

The stage of the design process when drawings and specifications are completed for construction bid purposes. It is preceded by the preliminary design stage and followed by the procurement phase.

Design – Preliminary

The transition from the schematic stage to the completion of design development. During this stage, ancillary space is developed, and dimensions are finalized. Outline specifications are developed into technical specifications; sections are delineated, and elevations are defined. Also known as design development.

Design – Schematic

Traditionally the first stage of the designer's basic services. In the schematic stage, the designer ascertains the requirements of the project and prepares schematic design studies consisting of drawings and other documents illustrating the scale and relationships of the project.

Digital Twin

A virtual model linked to physical elements, components, and processes on the actual construction site for the full project lifecycle.

Direct Costs

The field costs directly attributed to the construction of a project, including labor, material, equipment, subcontracts, and their associated costs.

Drawings

Graphic representations showing the relationships, geometry, and dimensions of the elements of the work.

E

Estimated Cost to Complete
The current estimate of the remaining costs to be incurred on a project at a specific point in time.

Estimated Final Cost
The anticipated cost of a project or project element when it is complete. The sum of the cost to date and the estimated cost to complete.

F

Fast Track
The process of dividing the design of a project into sub-phases in such a manner as to permit construction to start before the entire design phase is complete. The overlapping of the construction phase with the design phase.

Field Order
A written order issued at the site by the owner or CM to clarify or require the contractor(s) to perform work not included in the contract documents. A field order normally represents a minor change not involving a change in contract price or time and may or may not be the basis of a change order.

Final Completion
The date on which all the terms of the construction contract have been satisfied.

Float
Contingency time that exists on a scheduled activity. It represents the amount of time that activity may be delayed without effecting the end date of the schedule. It is measured by comparing the early start and late start, or early finish and late finish dates, of an activity.

Force Account
Directed work accomplished by the contractor outside of the contract agreement usually paid for on a time and material basis.

G

General Conditions
A section of general clauses in the contract specifications that establish how the project is to be administered. These may include, but are not limited to such items as temporary work, insurance, field offices, site security, scaffolding, hoists, signs, safety barricades, water boys, cleaning, dirt chutes, cranes, shanties, preparation for ceremonies including minor construction activity in connection therewith, temporary

toilets, fencing, sidewalk, bridges, first aid station, trucking, temporary elevators, special equipment, winter protection, temporary heat, water and electricity, temporary protective enclosures, field office and its related costs thereof such as equipment, furnishings and office supplies, progress photographs, messenger service, installation of owner furnished items, post and planking, general maintenance, subsoil exploration, refuse disposal, field and laboratory tests of concrete, steel, and soils, surveys, bench marks, and monuments, storage on-site and off-site of long lead procurement items, and miscellaneous minor construction work.

Green Globes

The Green Building Initiative (GBI) —The exclusive provider of Green Globes Building certifications in the US, it was developed as an evolution of the BREEAM international standard, and the first commercial building rating system based on an American National Standard (ANSI). Green Globes provides a choice of programs for green building guidance and assessment that includes Green Globes New Construction (NC), Green Globes Continual Improvement of Existing Buildings (CIEB), and Green Globes CIEB for Healthcare.

Green Star

Green Building Council of Australia (GBCA) has developed a variety of rating tools and a custom tool development service to measure and promote sustainability within Australia's built environment. Green Star is a comprehensive, national, voluntary environmental rating system that evaluates the environmental design and construction of buildings and communities. Green Star is transforming Australia's built environment by raising the awareness of the benefits of sustainable design, construction, and urban planning.

Guarantee

A legally enforceable assurance by the contractor, a third party, or both of satisfactory performance of products or workmanship during a specific period of time stated and included in the contract.

Guaranteed Maximum Price (GMP)

A contractual Form of Agreement wherein a maximum price for the work is established based upon an agreed to scope. Established with an understanding by the parties that the actual cost of the work could be more or less.

H

Hong Kong – Building Environment Assessment Method (HK BEAM)

This Hong Kong based method is a comprehensive environmental assessment scheme for buildings recognized by the HKGBC and was established in 1996, largely based on the UK Building Research Establishment's BREEAM system and was significantly upgraded in 2009 to become BEAM Plus. The BEAM Plus assessment scheme includes the six aspects of a project as follows: Site aspects; Materials aspects; Energy use; Water use; Indoor environmental quality; and Innovations and additions.

L

Leadership in Energy and Environmental Design (LEED)

Developed by the U.S. Green Building Council (USGBC), the LEED green building certification program offers a suite of rating systems that recognize projects that implement strategies for better environmental and health performance. LEED provides building owners and operators a framework for identifying and implementing practical and measurable green building design, construction, operations, and maintenance solutions.

Lien

A claim, encumbrance, or charge against or an interest in property to secure payment of a debt or performance of an obligation.

Lifecycle

The consecutive, interlinked stages of a product's production and use, beginning with raw materials acquisition and manufacture and continuing with its fabrication, manufacture, construction, use, and depletion, concluding with any of a variety of recovery, recycling, or waste management options.

Lifecycle Cost

All costs incident to the planning, design, construction, operation, maintenance, and demolition of a facility, or system, for a given life expectancy, all in terms of present value.

Liquidated Damages

An amount of money usually set on a per day basis, which the contractor agrees to pay the owner for delay in completing the work in accordance with the contract documents.

Long Lead Item

Material or equipment having an extended delivery time. Such items may be considered for early procurement and purchase under separate contract to facilitate on time completion of the project.

Low Bidder

The responsible bidder who has submitted the lowest bid, which is determined to be responsive to the request for bids for a division of work described in a bid document, proposal form, or contract.

Lump Sum Fee

A fixed amount (fee) that includes the cost of overhead and profit paid for work or a service, that does not change with the time the work takes or the scope of the services provided.

M

Master Schedule

An executive level summary schedule identifying the major components of a project, their sequence, and durations. The schedule can be in the form of a network, milestone schedule, or bar chart.

Milestone Schedule

A schedule representing important events along the path to project completion. Not all milestones are equally significant. The most significant are termed "major milestones" and usually represent the completion of a group of activities.

Multiple-Prime Contracts

Separate contractors contracting directly with the owner for specific and designated elements of the work.

N

Non-Conforming Work

Work that does not meet the requirements of the contract documents.

Notice of Award

The written notice of acceptance of the bid by the owner to a bidder stating that, upon compliance with the condition precedent enumerated therein, within the time specified, the owner will sign and deliver the contract.

Notice to Proceed (NTP)

A formal document or point in the project's lifecycle authorizing an individual or organization to commence work under its contract. The issuance of the NTP typically marks the end of the procurement phase and establishes the date for commencement of the contract time.

O

Owner Construction Management

A form of construction management that does not use an independent construction management organization as a team member. The owner performs all required construction management services with in-house staff.

Owner's Representative

The individual representing the owner on the project team.

P

Penalty

A punitive measure usually associated with failure to fulfill a contractual obligation.

Performance Bond

A pledge from a surety guaranteeing the performance of the work or payment of the bond amount to the obligee (owner or contractor) in the event of a default in performance of contractual obligations.

Phased Construction

An incremental approach to construction or design and construction. Each overlapping or sequential phase or element has a defined work scope.

Photogrammetry

A process that uses overlapping photographs of an object or area and converts them into 2D or 3D models.

Plans

Graphic representations showing the relationships, geometry, and dimensions of the elements of the work.

Post-Construction Phase

The period following substantial completion.

Pre-Design Phase

The period before schematic design commences during which the project is initiated, and the program is developed, the planning and conceptual phase.

Prime Contract

A direct contract with an owner. It can be a single contract and include the work specified for several contracts depending upon the division of work.

Prime Contractor

A contractor who has a contract with an owner.

Professional Services

Services provided by a professional or by an organization that has specific competence in a field of endeavor that requires professional (and technical) knowledge and capabilities and that meets recognized standards of performance.

Program Management

The practice of professional construction management applied to a capital improvement program of one or more projects from inception to completion. Comprehensive construction management services are used to integrate the different facets of the construction process, planning, design, procurement, construction, and activation, for the purpose of providing standardized technical and management expertise on each project.

Progress Meeting

A meeting dedicated to the subject of progress during any phase of project delivery.

Progress Payment

Partial payment of the contract amount periodically paid by the owner, upon approval by the CM, verifying that portions of the work have been accomplished.

Project

The total effort required in all phases from conception through design and construction completion to accomplish the owner's objectives. Also, defined as all work to be furnished or provided in accordance with the contract documents prepared by the designer.

Project Budget

The sum or target figure established to cover all the owner's costs of the project. It includes the cost of construction and all other costs such as land, legal and consultant fees, interest, and other project related costs.

Project Cost

The actual cost of the entire project.

Project Execution Plan (PxP)

A stand-alone document used for BIM rather than part of the PMP.

Project Management

As applied to a construction project, the use of integrated systems and procedures by the project team to accomplish design and construction. Project management is an integral function of construction management and includes the overall responsibilities that a CM must be capable of performing.

Project Management Plan (PMP)

A document prepared by the CM, and approved by the owner, which defines the owner's goals and expectations including scope, budget, schedule, and quality and the strategies to be used to fulfill the requirements of the project.

Project Procedures Manual (PPM)

A written, project-specific plan that outlines the project's scope, organization, and the specific approach to be undertaken to accomplish the various management tasks for the project.

Project Team

All project stakeholders engaged in completing the project and consisting of the owner, designer, CM, and prime contractors engaged in the design and construction.

Punchlist

A list made near the completion of the construction work indicating items of work that remain unfinished, do not meet quality or quantity requirements as specified or are yet to be performed and which must be accomplished by the contractor prior to completing the terms of the contract.

Q

Quality

The degree to which the project and its components meet the owner's expectations, objectives, standards, and intended purpose; determined by measuring conformity of the project to the plans, specifications, and applicable standards.

Quality Assurance (QA)

The application of planned and systematic methods to verify that quality control procedures are being effectively implemented.

Quality Control (QC)

The continuous review, certification, inspection, and testing of project components, including persons, systems, materials, documents, techniques, and workmanship to determine whether such components conform to the plans, specifications, applicable standards, and project requirements.

Quality Management (QM)

The process of planning, organization, implementation, monitoring and documenting of a system of policies and procedures that coordinate and direct relevant project resources and activities in a manner that will achieve the desired quality.

R

Record Drawings

Drawings (plans) prepared by the designer after construction is complete, that represent the work accomplished under the contract.

Recovery Schedule

The schedule that depicts action(s) and special effort(s) required to recover lost time in the approved schedule. It can depict activities of any member of the project team.

Request for Change Proposal

A written document issued by the CM to the contractor that describes a proposed change to the contract documents for purposes of establishing cost and time impacts. May also be known as a bulletin or request for quote.

Resiliency

The ability to withstand adverse impacts from natural and man-made threats.

S

Schedule of Values

A list of basic contract segments, in both labor and material, where each line item consists of a description of a portion of work and a related cost and the sum of the line items equals the total contract price. Generally used to determine progress payments to the contractor(s).

Scope

Identification of all requirements of a project or contract.

Scope Change

Changes that expand or reduce the requirements of the project during design or construction.

Shop Drawings

All drawings, diagrams, illustrations, schedules and other data which are specifically prepared by or for the contractor to illustrate some portion of the work and all illustrations, brochures, standard schedules, performance charts, instructions, diagrams and other information prepared by a supplier and submitted by the contractor to the designer or construction manager to demonstrate understanding of and compliance with the provisions of the contract documents.

Special Conditions (of the Contract for Construction)

See "Supplementary General Conditions."

Special Consultants

The designation for various professionals, including engineers, architects, designers, and other experts, who provide expertise in specialized fields.

Specifications

The detailed written descriptions of materials, equipment, systems, and required workmanship and other qualitative information pertaining to the work.

Start-Up

The period prior to occupancy when systems are activated and checked out, and the owner's operating and maintenance staff assumes the control and operation of the systems.

Subcontractor

Any individual, partnership, firm, corporation, or other business entity that has a contractual relationship with a contractor or any other subcontractor to furnish labor, equipment, or materials for performance of the work at the site.

Substantial Completion

The date, certified by the designer or CM or both, that the contractor has reached that stage of completion when the facility may be used for its intended purposes, even though all work is not fully completed.

Submittals

Transmittals of information as required by the contract documents.

Supplementary General Conditions

Additions or modifications to the general conditions, which are part of the bid documents or contract documents.

Sustainable

The condition of being able to meet the needs of present generations without compromising resources for future generations.

T

Testing

The application of specific procedures to determine if work has been completed in the prescribed manner and at the required levels of workmanship. See "Non-Conforming Work."

Trade Contractors

Construction contractors who specialize in providing or installing specific elements of the overall construction requirements of a complete project.

Trade-Off Study

The study to define the comparative values and risks of a substitution or exchange of a design component. The tradeoff can identify both monetary and functional values. Also known as an alternatives analysis.

U

USGBC

The U.S. Green Building Council is a non-profit organization devoted to shifting the building industry toward sustainability by providing information and standards on how buildings are designed, built, and operated. The USGBC is best known for the development of the Leadership in Energy and Environmental Design (LEED®) rating system and Greenbuild, a green building conference.

V

Value Engineering

A specialized cost control technique, which utilizes a systematic and creative analysis of the functions of a project or operation to determine how best to achieve the necessary function, performance, and reliability at the minimum lifecycle cost.

Virtual Reality (VR)

An interactive tool that fully immerses a user in a digital environment.

W

Warranty

Assurance by a party that it will assume stipulated responsibility for its own work for a given period of time.

Work

Contractor requirements to provide all labor, materials, tools, equipment, supplies, services, supervision, and performance for all operations as required by the contract documents.

Index

0-9

A

D

E

F

G

H

I

P

Q

R

S

Related Publications

2018 SALARY SURVEY

As part of its commitment to developing the workforce, CMAA conducted a salary survey of its members and credential holders in May 2018. The purpose of this research was to gather compensation and benefits information among those employed full-time in the construction industry.

CAPSTONE: AN INTRODUCTION TO THE CONSTRUCTION MANAGEMENT PROFESSION

This publication provides a basic understanding of construction management and the role of the construction manager.

CLAIMS MANAGEMENT GUIDELINES

The *Claims Management Guidelines* address the Construction Manager's roles and responsibilities regarding avoidance, mitigation, and resolution of disputes and claims between the owner and contractor(s) during the execution of construction projects.

CONTRACT ADMINISTRATION GUIDELINES

This manual addresses CM responsibilities during the execution of construction projects from concept to occupancy—developed as an expansion of the *Standards of Practice*.

COST MANAGEMENT GUIDELINES

Project cost management includes all those processes necessary to ensure that the project is completed within the approved budget. Cost management elements, the role of the construction manager with respect to cost management, and the use of various cost management tools are discussed for each phase of the project—developed as an expansion of the *Standards of Practice*.

PROJECT CLOSEOUT GUIDELINES

Project closeout is successful when all involved parties understand their closeout responsibilities based on the requirements outlined in the contract. Many of the closeout procedures are interconnected and often interdependent, so it's important that they are monitored and managed carefully. The *Project Closeout Guidelines* provide construction managers and the construction industry with general guidelines to successfully manage the closeout of construction projects.

QUALITY MANAGEMENT GUIDELINES

Quality management guidelines that should be integrated into every section of the construction management plan to maintain a focus on project quality—developed as an expansion of the *Standards of Practice*.

RISK MANAGEMENT GUIDELINES

The *Risk Management Guidelines* are intended to provide a generic framework to assist a professional construction manager in addressing risk and lessening the impact of risk events without limiting the methods and procedures by which a construction manager may provide those risk management services for a particular project or program.

SUSTAINABILITY GUIDELINES

CMAA's guide to implementing sustainable CM tools and processes throughout pre-design, design, procurement, construction, and post-construction project phases. Key topics include understanding the owner's sustainability goals and objectives; project delivery strategies; cost control; and administration details such as change management, QC inspection and testing documentation, and beneficial occupancy/substantial completion.

TIME MANAGEMENT GUIDELINES

Provides the CM practitioners and the industry at large with general guidelines on successful management of the "time" component of Projects—developed as an expansion of the *Standards of Practice*.